Daily Walk to Joy in the Midst

You Will Show Me the Path of Life;
in Your Presence is Fullness of Joy
(Psalm 16:11, NKJV)

ANNE M. DEL VECCHIO

Daily Walk to Joy in the Midst
Copyright © 2021 by Anne M. Del Vecchio

Unless otherwise stated, scriptures from New International Version Zondervan Bible Publishers

The Paradoxical Commandments are reprinted with the permission of the author. (c) Copyright Kent M. Keith 1968 Renewed 2001.

Scriptures taken from the Holy Bible, New International Version®, NIV®. Copyright © 1973, 1978, 1984, 2011 by Biblica, Inc.™ Used by permission of Zondervan. All rights reserved worldwide. www.zondervan.com The "NIV" and "New International Version" are trademarks registered in the United States Patent and Trademark Office by Biblica, Inc.™

All rights reserved. No part of this publication may be reproduced, distributed, or transmitted in any form or by any means, including photocopying, recording, or other electronic or mechanical methods, without the prior written permission of the author, except in the case of brief quotations embodied in critical reviews and certain other non-commercial uses permitted by copyright law.

ISBN
978-1-956161-38-0 (Hardcover)
978-1-956161-30-4 (Paperback)
978-1-956161-29-8 (eBook)

Dedication
To my husband, Gene, for his belief in me and constant encouragement to obey God and write. To my family for allowing me to honestly share parts of their story.

Acknowledgement
To our daughter, Monica, for her contributions to the book. To my son, Michael and his wife, Danielle, my writing cheer leaders. To Kathi Smith for her dedication to editing my manuscript. Her belief in the content being worthwhile was a strong motivator for me.

Truth and Fiction
All stories and names are fictional, except those relating to the author and family members. Our family, Gene, Michael, and Monica have chosen to be transparent in order to provide comfort for others struggling in similar circumstances.

Table of Contents

Prologue ix

Week 1	Packing for the Pilgrimage – Orientation	1
Week 2	Wilderness Wandering – Anne's Story	5
Week 3	God in Your Pocket – Jesus Story	9
Week 4	Mountain of Gloom – Misery	15
Week 5	Hard Life Hill – God Knows Me	18
Week 6	Faith Peak – The Great I Am	22
Week 7	Glorious View – He Cares	26
Week 8	Fellow Pilgrims – We Choose	30
Week 9	Joy in the Morning – Joy Defined	33
Week 10	Pit of Self-Pity – Woe is Me	37
Week 11	Piggy Playpen at Swampy Lake – Wallowing	41
Week 12	Pillars of Shame – Bad Me	45
Week 13	Valley of the Shadow of Death – Deep Grief	53
Week 14	Crying River – A Time to Weep	57
Week 15	His Staff – Out of Grief	61
Week 16	Expectation Pass – Reality	65
Week 17	Acceptance Grotto – It Is What It Is	70
Week 18	Hills of Hope – Belief Provides Hope	75
Week 19	Stinging Nettles – Pain is a Gift	79
Week 20	Sunlit Glade – Love Comes First	83
Week 21	Heart of a Pilgrim – Monica's Story	89

Week 22	Council Rock – Seek Wisdom 92
Week 23	Log Cabin Home – Build Your Home 98
Week 24	Disappointment Slew – Waiting 104
Week 25	Camp Fire Chat – Author's Struggles 108
Week 26	Grumbling Gulch – The Complaining Habit 113
Week 27	Contemplation Meadow – God is Good 119
Week 28	Lumbering Black Bear – Worries 125
Week 29	Thorny Bushes – The Angry Family 129
Week 30	Treachery Pass – Purpose and Pitfalls of Anger 133
Week 31	Cliffs of Anger – Conviction 137
Week 32	Abba's Trail – God's Anger Management 142
Week 33	Serenity Lake – Getting to Calm 147
Week 34	Pack Mules – Putting Off Putting On 152
Week 35	Mocha Machines and Other Weighty Stuff 157
Week 36	Resting in the Garden of God – Taking Rest 162
Week 37	Gurgling Brook – Children 166
Week 38	Baby's Breath – Heavy Decision 174
Week 39	Sweet Romance Falls – Being Loving 180
Week 40	Slippery Rocks – Do Not Weary 185
Week 41	Boundary Fence – No Abuse 189
Week 42	Sheltering Pines – Forgiveness 195
Week 43	Love Lookout – Pleasant Words 199
Week 44	Dark Forest – Sexual Sin 204
Week 45	Wild Honeysuckle – Love Making 209
Week 46	Broken Bridge – Finances 215
Week 47	Sunrise Glory – Cultivating Joy 223
Week 48	Meadow of Gladness – Gift of Gladness of Heart 228

Week 49 Heavenly Hot Springs – Pampering 233

Week 50 A Cup of Cool Water – Serving Others 238

Week 51 Lake of Still Waters – Resting in Jesus 243

Week 52 Happy Trails to You, Until We Meet Again – God's
          Love Letter and Epilogue 247

Epilogue 249
Note from the Author 253
Guidelines for Group Study 255

"*Come Walk with Me and Our Lord on A Journey to Joy*

Prologue

Week 1, Day 1

My childhood summers were spent roaming Tuolumne Meadows with my parents, high in the Sierra Mountains above Yosemite National Park. We bathed in ice cold springs, encountered bears, discovered artifacts from early settlers, and hiked on lonely trails singing hymns. My mother's favorite verse was, "I lift mine eyes to the hills, from whence cometh my help? My help cometh from the Lord, the Maker of heaven and earth," (Psalm 121:1–2 NKJV). She taught me to see my heavenly Father in the great wilderness, to find quietness of soul as I rested in Him.

Fast forward fifty years. When I sat down with thirty-five years of notes and journals, I had no vision how to congeal them into a cohesive book. I knew God called me to write yet could not get started. As I walked and waited in prayer, fretting and uncertain, without a clue, my favorite mountain vista came to mind. Gradually, the idea grew of taking my sisters in the Lord on an imaginary backpack trip to learn of God. Each morning as I sat in prayer and begged the Lord to speak through me, I was amazed as words flowed. Any drivel is my human "seeing dimly." Anything that is good, worthy of praise, or speaks to your heart, is from the Father, Son, and Holy Spirit. Praise be to God. "For now, we see in a mirror dimly, but then face to face. Now I know in part, but then I shall know just as I also am known," (1 Corinthians 13:12 NKJV).

Packing for the Pilgrimage

Do not merely listen to the word, and so deceive yourselves. Do what it says.

(James 1:22)

> Welcome, lady friends and sisters in Christ. I am so glad you decided to tackle the Mountain of Gloom with me, through many peaks and valleys, to refuge at the Lake of Still Waters. It is a long and treacherous journey so pack your pocket Bible, comfortable hiking boots, and a stout heart. We will walk along and chat about my life and yours. Are you ready? God is so good!

Orientation: This devotional leads with an imaginary back-packing trip over a mountain representing the journey of life. Our focus is leaning on God as our strength to become women who respond to life with joy, forgiveness and love instead of bitterness.

Be Still before the Lord, Ask for His Guidance, Contemplate His Word, Memorize, Act.

The book divides each lesson:

- ❖ Hiking story line. "I lift up my eyes to the hills; where does my help come from? My help comes from the Lord, the Maker of heaven and earth," (Psalm 121:1–2).
- ❖ Personal sharing, stories, or antidotes. "Praise be to the God and Father of our Lord Jesus Christ, the Father of compassion and the God of all comfort, who comforts us in our troubles, so that we can comfort those in any trouble with the comfort we ourselves have received from God," (2 Corinthians 1:3–4).

- ❖ Scripture lessons. "Taste and see that the Lord is good; blessed is the woman who takes refuge in him," (Psalm 34:6).
- ❖ Scripture to memorize or meditate on: Hide in My Heart: "I have hidden your word in my heart that I might not sin against you," (Psalm 119:11).
- ❖ Choose today. A call to decide. "Choose for yourselves this day whom you will serve… but as for me and my house, we will serve the Lord," (Joshua 24:15).
- ❖ Ponder or Journal. "Let love and faithfulness never leave you; bind them around your neck, write them on the tablet of your heart," (Proverbs 3:3).
- ❖ Action tools to carry out your faith: "Do not merely listen to the word, and so deceive yourselves. Do what it says," (James 1:22).
- ❖ Summary thoughts: Joy Trails

The stories and sharing are often autobiographic sharing the lessons of my journey. It is a story of heartache but, also, much joy.

Journaling is a great tool for those prone to write. Otherwise, sit quietly and ponder the journal questions. The "Choose Today" and "Action Tools" are vital for your growth. It is easy to read a scripture and then go about your day forgetting what you learned. The more you apply what you have learned to your daily life, the greater your transformation will be in the journey to joy. You need not follow every action tool. Neither should you beat yourself up if you implement a tool, then forget to continue. Choose those which best suit your need. Pray for your Father God to guide you. Be firm but gracious with yourself. Be willing to allow God to work within you to make the changes.

Note, when the generic "him" for mankind is used in scripture think "she" when applicable or write in your own name. Verses may show up several times over the course of the book…better to learn and memorize them.

> Well Ladies, did you bring a little-bitty journal and a pencil stub, bottles of water, food, bedroll and everything else on the list I sent you? It is my guess your packs weight about fifty pounds each. Heavy for this old girl! So, before we start the climb, let's go through our packs and trim out any excess, for instance, sunscreen and lip protection stay, lipstick goes back into the car. Only the necessities!
>
> **Prayer:** Here we are, Father God, ready to grow and learn from your word. Enable us to will and to act on your instructions through this journey. In Jesus name, Amen.

Hide in My Heart: (Memory Verse for the Week) "Do not merely listen to the word, and so deceive yourselves. Do what it says," (James 1:22).
Choose Today: As for me, I will serve the Lord.
Action Tool: Buy a journal. Plan to begin. If life interferes, restart the next day and the next.

Week 1, Day 2. Read: Psalm 121.
Be still, Pray, Ponder or Journal, Memorize, Act.
Journal: From where does your help come? Share your heart with God and listen to His instruction.
Action Tool: Look out a window to a tree top and the sky beyond. Symbolically, gather up the gunk of your personal stuff from your toes to your stomach to your head and throw it out that window to the God of the universe!

Week 1, Day 3. Read: 2 Corinthians 1:3–7.
Journal: When were you comforted by someone who has experienced similar sorrow? Whom have you comforted with the comfort you have received?
Action Tool: Be alert this week for the person God has set apart for you to comfort. Pray for them even before you know their name.

Week 1, Day 4. Read: Psalm 34:4-18 and Psalm 119:11.
Journal: When have you taken refuge in Jesus? Why should we memorize scripture (hide it in our heart)? Ask the Lord to give you a craving to be quiet with him.
Action Tool: Check-in. Are you being faithful to meet with the Lord most days? If you struggle to find time, ask the Lord to give you a strong desire for studying His word.

Week 1, Day 5. Read: Joshua 24:15.
Journal: What or whom most influences your decisions? Whom are you choosing to serve with your daily actions?
Action Tool: Reward yourself for completing 5 days of quiet time with the Lord despite being busy. Thank God for enabling you. "Alone and still before my Lord brings wisdom and rest."

Wilderness Wandering
Week 2, Day 1

> **Be merciful to me, Lord, for I am in distress; my eyes grow weak with sorrow, my soul and body with grief.**
> **(Psalm 31:9)**

> While you fill your water bottles, I'll give you my qualifications as your guide over the Mountain of Gloom. I'm an ordinary woman struggling through life just like you. Early on, I let God know my life plan demanded joy and laughter without pain or heartbreak. Apparently, God did not buy into my plan, and now, being over 60, I somehow-sort-a-think He is not going to. Even so, He has shown me through the sorrows how to experience joy amid life's struggles. Every day, I seek to learn more. Meanwhile, honoring God's instructions for the older women to teach the younger woman, I am delighted to walk along with you.

You are not alone in troubles and sorrows. Listen to a brief background of my story. Raised in a Christian home, in my early twenties, I rejected God. Then bounced in and out of a marriage. I renewed my faith in Jesus at age twenty-seven. Trusting the Lord for a Godly husband, I met Gene. On the third day of my honeymoon, my charming, new husband, a pillar of virtue in my eyes, lambasted me with unkind words. I felt God betrayed me and abandoned me to a lifetime in a miserable marriage. Within a year, I was pregnant. My son was born healthy after a difficult pregnancy. Though we were both delighted with our son, having a child did not cure Gene's anger or my misery. Subsequently, seven miscarriages devastated me with additional despair. Life continued to be a roller coaster of joy, laughter and love crashing into pain, angry words, and crying.

Gene and I were leveling out when we adopted our daughter, Monica, age three from an orphanage overseas. She did not understand how to function in a family. While I could handle a classroom of primary children, handling my new daughter was beyond me. My husband came home every night asking, "What is the Drama de Jour (of the day)?" I loved my family but could barely hold my head up each day. I envied everyone who appeared to have a wonderful family, felt very sorry for myself, and angry at God.

One year, my husband almost died from pleurisy, my son hospitalized with Hong Kong flu, and my mother fell on concrete resulting in brain damage. Meanwhile, I was dealing with hormonal changes from menopause. In addition, my daughter acted out daily. I plowed through tasks, then slept, and slept, and slept!

Finally, I visited a doctor for my exhaustion. He casually asked if I was under much stress. "Are you kidding? Stress is mild compared to what I am going through!" After my litany, he prescribed anti-depressants for post-traumatic stress syndrome. Even with medical help, it took God confronting me with scriptures to heal my mind and body. Instead of changing those around me, He taught me how to find joy during my painful circumstances. As He changed me, others in my family began to change as well.

When my children grew up and left home, God allowed another devastating circumstance. We invested heavily in real estate for retirement income. Along with many others, our real estate crashed big time the same year we retired on social security. Our home of twenty-three years was lost resulting in our living in a camper before moving far from family to a place less expensive. My response was illness, taking the stress into my body with shingles, vertigo, high blood pressure, weight gain and depression. So, God brought me new lessons of finding His joy amid hardship.

> Ok, enough of all that! It makes my life sound miserable... and, believe me, it often was. But that is not the whole story. Many blessings, joys, abundant love, a deep sense of peace and contentment have been my ultimate reward for the struggles. Although the "Drama de Jour" persists, my heart is free of bitterness, anger and depression. What a joy it is to walk with Jesus!

Prayer: Build our faith and trust in you, Father God, lighten our load and lift our weary souls. You are the only one who can do it, Abba, so we lay ourselves down before you, knowing you are faithful. Amen

Hide in My Heart: (Memory verse for the week) "Come to me, all you who are weary and burdened, and I will give you rest. Take my yoke upon you and learn from me, for I am gentle and humble in heart, and you will find rest for your souls for my yoke is easy and my burden is light" (Matthew 11:28–30).

Choose Today: Today I chose to follow God's word towards healing and wholeness no matter what my circumstance. He is wise and able to walk me through the fire.

Week 2, Day 2. Read: Psalm 31:7-9, 14-15.
Be still, Pray, Ponder or Journal, Memorize, Act.
Journal: What stresses your days and brings trouble or grief to your heart? Pour it out to your God in prayer and/or in your journal. Ask for the Lord to give insight into handling these issues.
Action Tool: Sit still before God. Gaze at something lovely. Praise God for at least 10 blessings in your life.

Week 2, Day 3. Read: Hebrews 10:10–25.
Journal: How does your heartache and stress stimulate you to actions unbeneficial for your well-being? Ask the Holy Spirit to inspire healthy ways to handle these feelings.
Joy Trail: Get up, dress nice, and go do something. Heartache often causes us to hunker down. Even if our actions are rote, doing something outside is healing.

Week 2, Day 4. Read: Psalm 84: 5, 11–12.
Journal: Our walk will not be blameless; that is why Jesus is our savior. Therefore, we are eligible to receive the strength of God on our pilgrimage. Pour out your need for His strength to be manifest in you through the Holy Spirit.
Action Tool: Build strength by taking a brisk 10-minute walk while practicing memorizing scripture.

Week 2, Day 5. Read: Matthew 11:28–30.
Journal: Pray for openness to conviction and a heart of repentance. How is God leading you to lay your burden upon Him and find rest for your soul?
Action Tool: Sing a praise song or hymn to the Lord, quietly in your mind or out loud.

God in Your Pocket
Week 3, Day 1

> **For God so loved the world that he gave his one and only son, that whosoever believes in Him shall not perish but have eternal life.**
>
> **(John 3:16)**

> Heading out on the Mountain of Gloom without God in your pocket is a bad idea. My little New Testament resides in my pack ready to show me the way. Yet, just having scriptures at ready is not enough. Having the Holy Spirit living in your person via Jesus, enables understanding of His teachings. If you have not yet accepted Christ as your Lord and Savior, or uncertain if you have, be assured, He is waiting for you to open the door to Him. Even if you are mature in the Lord, take time to refresh your walk with His story anew.

Long ago, the first woman, Eve, disobeyed the God of the Universe. Her husband, Adam, who was to be her protector did not intervene. In fact, he went along with Eve and bit the fruit she offered him from the tree of knowledge of good and evil. This is not a fairy tale. It is a true story. Ever since, each of us is given the same choice of trusting and obeying the one God or going our own way.

The Bible calls going our own way, sin. Everything from just a little selfishness to down-right evil is sin, all wrong behaviors in conflict with God's perfect plan for humankind. Just look around at the world and you will see wrong, hurtful, bad, and evil actions everywhere.

> For all have sinned and fall short of the glory of God.
>
> (Romans 3:23)

God knew the consequences of our wrongdoing would devastate us, but He gave us free-will. The consequences of our wrong choices bring about death. This death maybe experienced daily through misery within your soul. Then ultimately in physical death. However, life without Jesus separates us from the presence of God for all eternity.

> For the wages of sin is death.
> (Romans 6:23a)

God was not surprised when we chose the path of death. He knew we would before the creation of mankind. Why would he bother to create us in the first place then? Because it is His nature to create and to love. He made us in His image; giving us the ability to create and to love, therefore, gave us freedom of choice. Love is not love if one has no choice; it is just duty.

Even though He knew our wayward inclination, He is a God of holiness, of judgement and righteousness. Therefore, before the beginning of time, He also set out a plan to rescue us from our bad choices, our rebelliousness. God stepped into mankind with a way out of this death both for today, every day, and for eternity. He gave us Jesus Christ to take our wrong doings, upon himself so we need not pay the price. Why? Because God adopts us as His children and loves us deeply. When the whip of accusation strikes out against us, Jesus steps in and says, "Let me take the beating for you, you are free."

> But the gift of God is eternal life in Christ Jesus our Lord.
> (Romans 6:23b)

> But as many as received Him to them He gave the right to become children of God, even to those who believe in His name.
> (John 1:12)

> For God so loved the world (you and me) that He gave His one and only son, that whoever believes in Him should not perish but have everlasting life.
> (John 3:16)

> Jesus said to him, "I am the way, the truth, and the life. No one comes to the Father except through me."
> (John 14:6)

Everyone is welcome. God wants everyone to share His love and rescue but honors us with the choice. We must make our own decision to accept His gift of life.

> Behold, I stand at the door and knock. If anyone hears my voice and opens the door, I will come into him and dine with him and he with Me.
> (Revelation 3:20)

> For whoever calls on the name of the Lord shall be saved.
> (Romans 10:13)

God also gave us a counselor to be within us and guide us as we move forward with our daily choices as believers in Jesus Christ. Once we have asked Jesus into our life, he gives us the gift of the Holy Spirit to dwell within us, uplift and restore us day by day.

> And I will pray the Father, and he will send you another Helper, that He may abide with you forever – the Spirit of truth, whom the world cannot received, because it neither sees Him nor knows Him; but you know Him, for He dwells with you and will be in you.
> (John 14:17)

In addition, He has promised to provide *rest for your soul*.

> Come to me all you who are weary and burdened, and I will give you rest. Take my yoke upon you and learn from me, for I am gentle and humble in heart, and you will find rest for your souls.
> (Matthew 11: 28–29)

It is up to you. The choice is yours. Will you choose to be born anew into the family of God? Will you open your heart and mind to learning anew about the conviction, growth, peace, joy and victory he has for you? Simply, admit that you are hurt, mixed up, sinful and selfish, and then ask the Lord Jesus Christ to be your personal savior. Prayer is talking to God. No formality needed. Invite Him in, "Ok, God, if you are who you say you are, then you can have the mess I am. I accept Jesus as my rescuer and Lord (or use your own words)." Now, go tell someone you have invited Jesus into your life.

> If you confess with your mouth the Lord Jesus and believe in your heart that God has raised Him from the dead, you will be saved.
>
> (Romans 10:9)

Halleluiah! You are His! Whether you feel any different or not, you are now His and your life will begin to change. It is beyond comprehension that such a small moment will make a momentous difference in your life, yet if you were sincere in your invitation to Jesus, change will begin today.

> Most assuredly, I say to you, he who hears my word and believes in Him who sent Me has everlasting life, and shall not come into judgment, but has passed from death into life.
>
> (John 5:24)

> But these are written that you may believe that Jesus is the Christ, the Son of God, and that believing you may have life in His name.
>
> (John 20:31)

A new life is born, yours, in Christ. A new dawn is rising. Take heart, my sister, for though there are many mountains of gloom to climb in this life, the God of the Universe goes with you. Jesus the Savior and the Holy Spirit dwell within. You are not alone; you are part of the Family of God.

> Welcome, new ones, into the family of God. We are sisters indeed because we have the same father. Can't wait to tell family stories. Tomorrow, as we head out on the trail, we will talk more. Enjoy a soft "real bed" here in the lodge because the ground out there is hard. We have tough trails ahead. God bless you, fellow journeyers. Sweet dreams.

Prayer: Lord, reveal what I need to hear and understand this day about your relationship to me. Direct me to the scriptures needed at this moment in my life. I wait for you. Amen.
Hide in My Heart: "For God so loved the world he gave his one and only son, that whosoever believes in Him shall not perish but have eternal life," (John 3:16).
Choose Today: I choose Jesus!

Week 3, Day 2. Read: Romans 6:23.
Journal: How have you experienced death (sadness, despair, ending of relationships, etc.) during your life? What resulted from the wrongful behaviors of others? What part by your own wrongful actions?
Action Tool: Make a list of your typical prideful, arrogant, selfish, woe is me, or hurtful behavior. Write it on a scrap of paper. Wad up the paper, then burn it.

Week 3, Day 3. Read: John 1:12, John 3:16 and John 14:6.
Journal: If you have not already done so, pray about opening your heart and mind to Jesus. Ask Him to be your Lord and Savior. If you are already His child, ask Him to ignite the flame of the Holy Spirit within you, giving you a new passion for His life in you.
Action Tool: Yesterday you burned your "sins" symbolically. Today cup your hands before you, close your eyes and receive the forgiveness of Jesus.

Week 3, Day 4. Read: Romans 10:9.
Journal: Have you spoken about your faith as a believer? If you are new to accepting Jesus, have you told someone? Write your "testimony" (your story of coming to belief in Jesus).
Action Tool: Call, email, or text someone about your new or renewed faith.

Week 3, Day 5. Read: John 5:24 and John 20:31.
Journal: God assures you a place in heaven through Jesus. He, also, provides joy, strength, and other fruits of the spirit while you are alive. Do you believe this? What does this assurance mean to you?
Action Tool: Read Psalm 66 and claim it for your own.

Mountain of Gloom

Week 4, Day 1

> **I have told you these things, so that in me you may have peace. In this world you will have trouble. But take heart! I have overcome the world.**
>
> **(John 16:33)**

> Morning, Lady Friends? Observe the narrow trail up that ominous dark mountain surrounded by a dense grey fog? That, gals, is The Mountain of Gloom. The hardest part of the entire journey is facing the steep climb of our bad habits and emotions, so let's get started. Give each other a hand. Set those packs on a rock, then heft them up on your shoulders. Whew! Ready? Head out!

The weather this morning is reminiscent of the gloom residing in my mind. Maybe you can relate. "My eyes flicker open glimpsing briefly a foggy, cold, slate-grey gloom. Grey overcast skies, not enough money, kids making bad decisions; husband grumpy… grey is the color of my mood… life without flavor, without victory, joyless. Even when skies are blue for everyone else, they are grey for me. I am lost in a gloom cloud, walking through mud, every step labor-some and exhausting. Bed and sleep are my greatest friends."

Life is unfair. My pain may be minuscule compared to your circumstances; even so it is my pain. I am the one suffering through it, so my hurt seems huge to me. Despite my faith and family who love me, I woke morning after morning depressed and joyless. Were you to hear more details of my circumstances, you would agree I own the right to be depressed. Yet, I refused to live in a Grey Fog on the Mountain of Gloom. Tempting as it was to bury deep in the covers wrapping myself in the dark comfort of the hurt in my heart, I refused.

I learned through the seasons of waking up to a grey fog that seeking joy amid life's troubles is a choice! Gladness of heart is a gift of God, yet whether I receive that gift daily is my choice. It is a choice I still must make every single day. Life is unfair, so be it. I asked the Lord to open my eyes to joy despite the sorrows.

Have you ever dwelt in a dense grey fog? Since you are climbing Gloom Mountain with me, it is my guess your answer is yes. So, here are recommendations:

- ❖ Most important of all, throw yourself on the mercy of God and pour out your hurt to Him.
- ❖ Meet with Him daily to pray, read, journal, cry, rejoice and learn trust.
- ❖ Memorize scripture to use as a balm to your wounds and medicine to your soul.
- ❖ Be involved with a women's Bible study that includes sharing and prayer.
- ❖ Seek Christian counsel based on the scriptures. Sift any advice through the word of God.
- ❖ Be gentle with yourself yet firm with no excuses.

Christian author, Tim Hansel has a saying that speaks volumes, "Pain is inevitable; misery is optional." What do you choose in the midst of your now?

> I see the fog is lifting, but gals, look ahead. Oh my! Walking in from the trail head was a stroll through the park, despite the grey, compared to what comes next. Look at those granite boulders piled high. That is Hard Life Hill, the only way over the Mountain of Gloom. Slow and steady, we can do this, sisters.

Prayer: O Lord our God, as we turn our hearts towards finding your joy despite life struggles, enable us to grow deeper awareness of you and the ability to make Godly choices. Amen.

Hide in My Heart: "I have told you these things, so that in me you may have peace. In this world you will have trouble. But take heart! I have overcome the world" (John 16:33).

Week 4, Day 2. Read: Isaiah 40:28-31.
Journal: Ask God to give insight into your personal mountain of gloom and his directions for going forward. How does your gloom manifest itself?
Action Tool: Make a note of the "next right step for you" from the bullets in this week's lesson.

Week 4, Day 3. Read: John 16:33.
Journal: Beseech our living God for direction as to how you can "take heart".
Action Tool: Take the "next right step" today. Listen to what God is placing on your heart.

Week 4, Day 4. Read: Psalm 20.
Journal: What further steps is God asking of you to conquer this gloom.
Action Tool: Chase gloom away by taking a brisk 10-minute walk while practicing memorizing a scripture.

Week 4, Day 5. Read: Ephesians 3: 14-21 Paul praying for you.
Journal: Pour out your own prayer to your Father God.
Joy Trail: Live today! If you concentrate on your regrets and sorrows of yesterday, or long for a different tomorrow, you will miss out on every "today".

Hard Life Hill
Week 5, Day 1

> **Each heart knows its own bitterness, and no one else can share its joy.**
>
> **(Proverbs 14:10)**

> One foot in front of another, one step at a time, we can make it up and over Hard Life Hill. Dig your staff firm into the hill using it as a third leg. That's it. When we get to those boulders, we'll take off our packs and tie on ropes. Once we have climbed the boulders, we'll pull up the packs. It appears unsurmountable, gals, doesn't it? But don't give in just yet, remember one step at a time.

Have any of you ladies ever sat in church thinking…where is the victory, the joy and peace promised by so many scriptures? I believe. I am a Christian. Why is my reality so different from what I am "supposed to feel" as a Christian? Why is life so hard? Why am I not experiencing the "peace of God", "rest for the weary", "joy of the Lord", and "contentment in all circumstances"? Have you ever secretly struggled with these thoughts?

As you heard, my circumstances were tumultuous and painful. I was singing about victory in Jesus, yet my emotions did not reflect victory. Sitting in my pew, my mind screamed, "How?" How do I experience victorious Christian living amid difficult circumstance and God's apparent indifference? Right here, right now, where it matters most in day to day living. What about you? Are you like me or am I the only one? Since you joined me on this hike, I am confident you understand.

God doesn't operate like a Santa Claus. Wish he did! My prayers clearly list my needs and wants. Therefore, I earnestly hope He will fulfill my list… for Christmas, my birthday, Mother's Day, what about on Wednesday… any Wednesday? I don't care. I want what I want. "And Father God," I plead reasonably, "It's all good Godly stuff so you should say yes".

Here is one list:

- ❖ My husband's anger and depression to go away.
- ❖ My daughter to make good decisions.
- ❖ A job for my son.
- ❖ A few more years for my aging mom.

See, Journey Friends, not selfish. It is good stuff. Yes, I accept when I die, I'll have eternal life. But today, while I am still alive, what good is God to me? Selfishly speaking, because let face it, we are all selfish. God answered my misery by convicting me with scriptures. He took me to Psalms.

> I, the Lord your God, have searched you and know you. I know your sitting down and rising up; I understand your thoughts afar off. I comprehend your path and your lying down; I am acquainted with all your ways. For there is not a word on your tongue, but behold, I your Lord, know it altogether. I have hedged you behind and before and laid my hand upon you. Such knowledge is too wonderful for you; it is high, you cannot attain it.
> Where can you go from my Spirit? Or where can you flee from my presence? If you ascend into heaven, I am there; if you make your bed in hell, behold, I am there. If you take the wings of the morning and dwell in the uttermost parts of the sea, even there my hand shall lead you and my right hand shall hold you.
> If you say, "Surely the darkness shall fall on me and the light become night around me." Indeed, I your God say, the darkness shall not hide from me but the night shines as the day; the darkness and the light are both alike to me. For I formed your inward parts; I covered you in your mother's womb. For you are fearfully and wonderfully made; you are one of my marvelous works. Your frame was not hidden from me when you were made in secret and skillfully woven together. My eyes saw your

substance, being yet unformed. And in my book, they all were written, the days fashioned for you, when as yet there were none of them.

(Psalm 139: 1–16)

Just as with Job in the Bible, God did not give me direct answers to my questions. HE REDIRECTED ME TO WHO HE IS! He wanted me to ACCEPT that He knows my makeup from birth to death and nothing in my life goes without His involvement. Bad and good circumstances are still in His hands. Even the horrible, unspeakable events, though not his choice for us are still not beyond his presence. Though decisions of evil man and woman bring suffering, God is still there for me and you. Will I choose to rest and allow Him to do his work in me, despite the trouble of my days?

For I am persuaded that neither death nor life, nor angels nor principalities nor powers, nor things present nor things to come, nor height nor depth, nor any other created thing, shall be able to separate us from the love of God which is in Christ Jesus our Lord.

(Romans 8:38–39)

The first step is to align yourself with the Creator of the Universe, your God, and Savior. Count on Him and His love to work within the weighty circumstances of your life to mold you into a woman of God. Because we live in a fallen, sinful world, where selfishness and evil exist, it will not be easy, but He will do great things if you are willing. Choose to walk with your God through the sorrows.

> Trusting God to change my darkness to daylight, my gloom ever-so-slowly lifted. Since sleep was my escape, my husband woke me each morning by handing me my Bible and a cup of tea. Reading the word and journaling, focused me on life instead of death (depression). Ok, gals, let's pitch camp here on Hard Life Hill. The morning was gloomy, but I see a hint of a spectacular sunset.

Prayer: O Lord, we are so weak. Thank you for loving us anyway. Open our minds and hearts, Lord, to experience deep within our being, how great is your love for us. Amen.

Hide in My Heart: "For I am persuaded that neither death nor life, nor angels nor principalities nor powers, nor things present nor things to come, nor height nor depth, nor any other created thing, shall be able to separate me from the love of God which is in Christ Jesus our Lord" (Romans 8:38–39).

Choose Today: I choose to seek you, my God and Father to get over "Hard Life Hill".

Week 5, Day 2. Read: Job 38:1 to 42:6.
Journal: What do you hold against God for your circumstance? How does it seem to you that He is unfair or uncaring in your life? Confess these things to our almighty God.
Action Tool: Praying scripture. Get on your knees and cry out loud in prayer, "Endow my heart with wisdom, Lord, and give understanding to my mind," (Job 38:36).

Week 5, Day 3. Read: Romans 8:38–39.
Journal: Do you really feel loved by God? Do you believe he will never forsake you? Journal your real, true feelings.
Action Tool: Praying scripture. Bow your head and claim with your heart, "The Lord is my strength and my shield; my heart trusts in him, and I am helped," (Psalm 28:7).

Week 5, Day 4. Read: Psalm 139.
Journal: Write out verses from Psalm 139: 23–24 as a prayer for yourself.
Action Tool: Praying scripture. Look to the heavens and read aloud the verses you wrote in your journal,

Week 5, Day 5. Read: Psalm 86.
Journal: Write verses from this Psalm which jump out at you. Underline them in your Bible and date them as God's word for you.
Joy Trail: Eyes up. Look to God for strength and blessings, even if all you can manage today is to pray "Help!"

Faith Peak
Week 6, Day 1

> **I do believe, help me overcome my unbelief.**
>   **(Mark 9:24)**

> Rise and shine, Ladies, I've made you a hot mocha on my portable espresso machine. We hike up Faith Peak today. While you sip your mocha relax, close your eyes, and listen.

Picture a white sandy beach with azure water lapping at the shores and palms trees swaying in the breeze. You may be on this barren Mountain of Gloom, yet I guarantee you can visualize this beach. You *believe* it exits because photos testify that tropical beach splendor is real.

Now, think of a mother holding her sleeping infant as she lies on a beach lounge. Do you see the love in her face? Love being an emotion, not an object, this is as close as you can get to holding love in your hand. You *believe* in love because you observe evidence of love in action.

Our God is invisible; His interaction in our life subtle; His voice a still small whisper. How can I "believe" when I cannot see him? When I do not "feel" Him? Doubts can creep in. Perhaps, He just created the world and then went on His own way. Perhaps, it makes no difference if I follow Him or not? Perhaps, if I don't believe in Him, then God, doesn't exit.

Our belief in God is often so shallow and fickle, increasing and waning with every circumstance. We *believe* in a tropical beach because we have seen pictures of it; we *believe* in love because we have seen and/or experienced the results of love. We can also believe in our Father God, the Son Jesus and the Holy Spirit because of testimonies and evidence of the unseen God:

❖ Human witnesses rarely agree, yet scriptures written over 2000 years, by many authors agree on one message. The theme,

predictions, and fulfillment are consistent, speaking of a God who created, loves and redeems his people.
- ❖ Testimonies of witnesses in scripture and other ancient secular documents prove the reality of the historical Jesus.
- ❖ The created earth with infinite variety that (without man's interference) works together seamlessly speaks of God himself.
- ❖ The intuitive moral standard held by all mankind reflects love and a desire for rightness. Though this standard may be exhibited differently or ignored completely by individuals, all societies have moral standards that are essentially laws of loving one another. All people express a need for love and feel an emptiness without it. Where did this come from? This is beyond matter and chemicals; it is the image of God within us.

Whenever hardships come our way or evil attacks us, our human tendency is to doubt God existence or concern for us.

A father seeking healing for his son spoke to Jesus, "If you can do anything, take pity on us and help us."

"If I can?" said Jesus, "Everything is possible for him who believes."

> Immediately, the boy's father exclaimed, "I do believe, help me overcome my unbelief.
> (Mark 9:22b–24).

On your feet, fellow hikers, time to power up Faith Peak.

God's said to Moses, "I am who I am!" He is God, the beginning, and the end, the ruler of the universe. He is boss-man, emergency medical team, professor, king, nurse, mother, father, judge, jury, servant, psychologist, mother-earth and trash hauler. He is the deciding authority over us in every aspect of our lives, *whether or not we believe in Him, whether or not we accept it*. He is. He is also our caregiver, lover of our soul, nurturer, and savior, *whether or not we believe or accept it*.

> Because what may be known of God is manifest in them (mankind) for God has shown it to them. For since the

creation of the world His invisible attributes are clearly seen, being understood by the things that are made (all of nature), even His eternal power and Godhead, so they (mankind) are without excuse.

(Romans 1: 19-20)

God is an all-knowing authority who in some mysterious way works together with your free will, involving himself in our circumstances. You cannot force him to do it your way. Yet he is powerful and helpful.

So, what good is this God to us today? Well, since life guarantees we will have our share of suffering, we might as well link into the great advisor of the universe. Like the doubting father in the gospel of Mark 9:24, we can cry out, "I do believe, help me overcome my unbelief." Then we have immediate access to God the Father, Jesus, the emergency rescue officer, the Holy Spirit, our personal wise counselor, and the guidebook for life, the Bible. Otherwise, we go it alone. My choice is to believe no matter what. What's yours?

> Girls, I'm about winded. What do you say, I sit a spell and you go on ahead up Faith Peak? My old bones gotta' take it slow until I get adjusted to the high altitude. Leave your packs here. I'll keep an eye on them. You'll discover a glorious view from the top; worth the effort.

Prayer: Lord, I believe, help my unbelief. We want so much to believe and trust in you but so often doubt. You say no one comes to the Father except that you draw them, so I know you understand. Create in me a heart fully given to faith in you. Thank you, Father. Amen.

Hide in My Heart: "Now fear the Lord and serve him with all faithfulness.... But if serving the Lord seems undesirable to you, then *choose for yourselves this day whom you will serve*.... But as for me and my household, we will serve the Lord" (Joshua 24:14–15).

Choose Today: I choose you, Father God.

Week 6, Day 2. Read: Mark 9:24.
Journal: What are your doubts about God, Jesus and the Holy Spirit? When has it seemed God was unwilling to help?
Action Tool: Pray scripture. Bend your head in humbleness and let the Lord know, "I do believe, help me overcome my unbelief" (Mark 9:24).

Week 6, Day 3. Read: Psalm 142, David's lament.
Journal: Write out verses Psalm 142:3 and 5.
Joy Trails: Choose to Believe. We can choose to believe our doubts or choose to believe our God. Strength and wisdom come in acting on our belief that God is.

Week 6, Day 4. Read: Romans 1:19–20.
Journal: Consider the intricacies of nature, and the ability of man for love and kindness. How do you see God manifested (revealed)?
Action Tool: Go outside today, no matter the weather, and notice the intricacies and beauty of what God has created.

Week 6, Day 5. Read: Psalm 145.
Journal: Write out the verses into your journal from this Psalm that call out to you. Underline them in your Bible and date them as words God has given for you.
Action Tool: On an index card write this affirmation. "Today I choose to serve my God and Lord; He shall deal bountifully with me." Post this card on your bathroom mirror. Read it every time you pass by.

Glorious View
Week 7, Day 1

> **I will sing of the mercies of the Lord forever; with my mouth will I make known, your faithfulness to all generations.**
>
> **(Psalm 89:1)**

> Is that singing I hear? Must be the gals coming back from Faith Peak. Guess the Lord opened their hearts to the one worthy of praise. Hey, joyful ones. Did you meet King David up there? From your countenance, I bet you did. He hangs out on Faith Peak ready to share with pilgrims. Tell me, what did he say?

King David in his writings reveals that our lament about God not caring, not listening, and not acting on our timeline, is nothing new. David was a number-one whiner for a season of his life. Samuel anointed him to be the next king when he was approximately sixteen. David was kind and faithful to the current king, Saul, even singing him goodnight lullabies. After David killed Goliath and defended Israel becoming number-one warrior, King Saul got jealous. Subsequently, Saul persecuted and pursued David intending to kill him. Not light-hearted living or at all what David expected when chosen by God. Listen to King David.

> Why do You stand afar off, O Lord? Why do You hide in times of trouble? How long, O Lord? Will you forget me forever? How long will You hide Your face from me? As the deer pants for the water brooks, so my soul pants for you, O God. My tears have been my food day and night, while they continually say to me, "Where is your God?" When I remember these things, I pour out my soul within me. For I used to go with the multitude; I went with them

to the house of God, with the voice of joy and praise, with
the multitude that kept a pilgrim's feast.
(Psalm 10:1, Psalm 13:1, Psalm 42:1, 3–4).

Paraphrased, "I used to be happy and have joy. Now look at me, God; why aren't you fixing this?" Then King David shared a shift in thinking; the shift required of us when we wake up on the mountain of gloom.

> Why are you downcast, O my soul? And why are you disquieted within me? Hope in God, for I shall yet praise Him, the help of my countenance and my God.
> (Psalm 42:11)

Our God is a Father to whom we can pour out our heart without condemnation. God won't get bored, weary or impatient with your human frailties. Our friends tire of our moaning; He does not. God is the one who can intercede in our circumstances. He is the one who in due time will turn our "wailing into dancing". Therefore, vital to our securing any measure of peace and joy during the seasons of pain is holding strong to "I will yet praise Him, the help of my countenance and my God!"

> I will lift up my eyes to the hills, from whence comes my help. My help comes from the Lord who made heaven and earth. He will not allow your foot to be moved. He who keeps you will not slumber. The Lord is your keeper; the Lord is your shade at your right hand. The sun shall not strike you by day, nor the moon by night. The Lord shall preserve you from all evil; He shall preserve your soul. The Lord shall preserve your going out and your coming in from this time forth, and even forevermore.
> (Psalm 121)

Pour out your thoughts to our God. Be authentic with him, not fake.

> The Lord is my strength and my shield; my heart trusts in him, and I am helped.
> (Psalm 28:7)

> Good to see your spirits have picked up, ladies. Spending time on Faith Peak amplifies hope. Even on the Mountain of Gloom you discovered faith. Isn't the view from Faith Peak glorious? Join me on a comfortable rock and bask in the joy of the Lord for a while?

Make a joyful shout to the Lord all the lands! Serve the Lord with gladness; come before His presence with singing. Know that the Lord, He is God; it is He who has made us, not we ourselves; we are his people and the sheep of His pasture. Enter His gates with thanksgiving and into His courts with praise, be thankful to Him and bless His name. For the Lord is good; His mercy is everlasting, and His truth endures to all generations.

(Psalm 100)

Prayer: Father God, thank you for including honest descriptions of flawed people in your word; people just like us. It is encouraging to know we are not the only ones struggling. Thank you, Lord, for being here, right now, for me. Amen.

Hide in My Heart: "Why are you downcast, O my soul? And why are you disquieted within me? Hope in God, for I shall yet praise Him, the help of my countenance and my God (Psalm 42:11)."

Choose Today: I choose to look not down in despair or straight ahead at my own abilities but up to my God.

Week 7, Day 2. Read: Psalm 42.
Journal: What causes you to look at the circumstances or your own abilities rather than up at the Lord?
Action Tool: Eyes-Up. Remember those little motivational star charts your elementary teachers used? Well, since we are children at heart, today's homework is a motivational chart.

❖ Choose a place to keep a daily record (on a calendar, your journal, or even an emoji on a notepad in your phone.)

- ❖ Each morning record how you did the day before. Did you walk around looking down, depressed, worried, or anxious? Then draw a downcast eye (half circle with lashes at the bottom) or sad emoji.
- ❖ Did you depend on your own strength? Then draw a looking straight-ahead eye (oval with a dot for the eye) or expressionless emoji.
- ❖ Or did you look up to the Lord, depending on him to get you through and praising Him despite the circumstance? Draw a looking up eye (half circle with lashes at the top) or joyful emoji.
- ❖ Sometimes, you may need several eyes for the same day. Keep this record for at least one month or longer. Your goal is more eyes-up than down.

Week 7, Day 3. Read: Psalm 121.
Journal: How have you experienced God protecting you and guiding you? If you cannot think of His interaction on your behalf, pray that He will open your eyes, for He most certainly has done so.
Action Tool: Eyes Up. Record your "eyes" from yesterday.

Week 7, Day 4. Read: Habakkuk 3:17-19.
Journal: Write you own psalm by filling in the blanks.
Though _____ does not _____,
And this _____ does not _____,
I shall yet _____.
I will rejoice in Jesus my Savior.
Action Tool: Eyes Up. Record your "eyes" from yesterday.

Week 7, Day 5, Read: Psalm 100.
Journal: In what ways, this week, can you enter His gates with thanksgiving and praise?
Action Tool: Eyes Up. Record your "eyes" from yesterday.

Fellow Pilgrims
Week 8, Day 1

> **The wise woman builds her house, but with her own hands the foolish one tears hers down.**
>
> **(Proverbs 14:1)**

> While you were climbing up Faith Peak, I met a few interesting fellow pilgrims. You may have noticed a teenage girl, outlandishly dressed, speaking profanity, and a young single mom trying desperately to climb the mountain with three little ones in tow. Did you see a plump woman in stylish hiking clothes huffing one slow step at a time, her head high and haughty? An older woman sat with me for a while pouring out her bitter regrets of all her years. It would be fascinating to observe the transformation of each woman as she comes down from Faith Peak. This reminds me of two stories...

As a young woman, I was seated in an airplane behind two women about age forty and seventy-five. The elderly lady griped and complained in a shrill voice. The seat was too hard, the coffee lukewarm, and on and on. The younger woman, her daughter, criticized her mother while apologizing to the stewardess. "You're just a nasty old woman. I shouldn't take you anywhere!" "I'm sorry; she's just a miserable person." It continued loudly until the mom fell asleep.

Watching and listening, I pictured of the years of life stripping away outer garments of civility. Our body loses its youthful beauty. We no longer need to impress employers. Our friends die off. Our ability to do things and go places falls away. Today loses its sharpness and pain frequents our joints. In the process, we distill to the *real person inside*, no longer required to put on a front. The daughter was polite and pleasant to the stewardess but not so to her mom. The mom had become a bitter old woman. It was clear that the daughter was well on her way to becoming the same.

The second story comes from a stack of letters found recently, written by my mother to my father during their courtship in 1943. In the first letter, they were dating. As the letters continued, they got engaged, then married. Shortly after marriage they lived apart due to illness of my mother. From dewy-eyed girl in-love to newlyweds with friction, to anger, hurt and jealousy on my father's part because of the separation, my mom is unveiled in these letters. They never resolved hurts of those early days due to their "stow-it" tendencies. Even so, my parents with a heart for the Lord created a loving home for us and many others whom they took in. Forgiveness and love were characteristic of my mother. She chose to forgive despite many trials, hurts and disappointments. As an 80-year-old woman with brain damage due to a severe fall, it was common to hear others comment, "What a dear sweet woman." She offered a helping hand whenever possible even with her limited abilities. When the outer body deteriorated, all that remained was the true person, a woman of God.

The point of these stories is that we have a choice every day to believe our God can work within us and yield to his molding. We also can choose not to believe and not to yield. If we allow the hardships of life to cultivate bitterness we lose so much. Everyone suffers hardships. With God's work in you, you can become better instead of bitter. You can distill to inner loveliness. Who do you want to be as a wizen old lady?

After years of hard life experiences, when new acquaintances hear my story, their most common comment is my lack of bitterness. It didn't come automatically; it came with surrender and God's work within me. Praise His name! If He can do it for me, He can do it for you too, dear one.

> Shall we set up camp for the night, girls? There is a pleasant glade just over yonder with a bubbling brook to sing us to sleep.

Prayer: Lord, keep us from bitterness of the soul. Work mold us into your likeness being ever more faithful, resilient, forgiving and strong. Create in us a receptive spirit to your instruction. May we each distill into a beautiful aged "woman after God's own heart" through the power of Jesus Christ. Amen.

Hide in My Heart: "I will give you a new heart and put a new spirit in you; I will remove from you your heart of stone and give you a heart of flesh, (Ezekiel 36:26)."

Choose Today: I choose to become a woman of God with a desire for a new spirit and a heart of flesh (loving, feeling, forgiving).

Week 8, Day 2. Read: Proverbs 14:1.

Journal: How can our words and actions tear apart our house, home, family? What actions and words will build our home? Whom do you know who has walked with God through hardship without bitterness?

Action Tool: Seek an elderly woman of God in the church. Ask her to share how she saw, over time, God's hand working all circumstance together for good. Your conversations with older believers give evidence of God's work. It is your proof of an invisible God. Lock these pictures in your heart as you become a woman after God's own heart. It will take a lifetime.

Week 8, Day 3. Read: Ezekiel 36:26.

Journal: What bitterness have you allowed? What robs you of peace? What signs have you seen of God giving you a new heart?

Action Tool: Paste a picture of yourself on an index card. Write today's scripture below your picture. A promise God has for you. Your job is be willing to allow open heart surgery.

Week 8, Day 4. Read: 1 Peter 4:7–19.

Journal: How is the Lord asking you to administer grace?

Action Tool: Circle the words in today's scripture that jump out with meaning for you.

Week 8, Day 5. Read: Proverbs 31: 10–31.

Journal: Write out a prayer asking God to grow you into a woman of strength, wisdom and dignity.

Action Tool: No one is a perfect woman; each of us can continue to grow. Choose one thing to do different today to become better not bitter. For instance, pick up the pair of pants your husband dropped on the floor and pray with thanksgiving for this loved one.

Joy in the Morning
Week 9, Day 1

Weeping may remain for a night, but joy comes in the morning.
(Psalm 30:5b)

> Sleep well, friends? The sound of a bubbling brook is God's lullaby and the forest an orchestra for the wearied soul. Be still for a while; listen to the music of His unspoiled creation.
>
> Shout for joy to the Lord, all the earth, burst into jubilant song with music; make music to the Lord with the harp, with the harp and the sound of singing, with trumpets and the blast of the ram's horn—shout for joy before the Lord, the King. Let the sea resound, and everything in it, the world, and all who live in it. Let the rivers clap their hands, let the mountains sing together for joy.
>
> (Psalm 98: 4-8)

As we seek to find joy in-the-midst of struggles and sorrows, we need to understand the meaning of joy as expressed in the word of God. Review these definitions:

> <u>English Dictionary:</u> Joy. 1a: the emotion evoked by well-being, success or good fortune or by the prospect of possessing what one desires, b: the expression or exhibition of such emotion: gaiety. 2a: a state of happiness or felicity: bliss, 3a: a source or cause of delight.*
>
> Blithe: A happy lighthearted character of disposition.*

---

*   Webster Dictionary

> Glad: Marked by a feeling of being pleased, satisfied gratification, experiencing pleasure or joy.*
> Greek: Gladness, calm, delight, calmly happy or well-off.*
> Hebrew: Blithesomeness or glee, exceeding gladness, mirth, pleasure, rejoicing, welcome, goodness, loud voice of rejoicing, proclamation, singing, triumph, to cheer up, brighten up, make merry.**

The dictionary definition of joy is beyond comprehension when daily pain or depression enters our home. In fact, this kind of emotion would be insincere, phony, emotionally crippling and bizarre in the face of sorrow. So how in the world can we have joy in the midst? Let us dig deeper into the Hebrew and Greek terms translated as "joy" in our English Bible. In both ancient languages the elements of exceptional delight, gladness, even mirth, were a part of the meaning. However, in many Bible verses the ancient word translated as our word "joy" is defined as:

> Joy: Devine influence upon the heart and its reflection in life, acceptable, gratitude, pleasure, thank-worthy.**

In various contents of scripture, it also means:

> Joy: Calmly glad, a sense of well-being, marked by a feeling of being pleased or satisfied gratification, gratitude, acceptable, welcome, to cheer up.*

In Nehemiah 8:10b, "Do not grieve, for the joy of the Lord is your strength" the word joy means "Godhead". Paraphrased this verse says, "Do not grieve, for the Godhead himself, delight and pleasure in Him, is your strength."

---

*   Webster Dictionary
** Strong's Exhaustive Concordance of the Bible, Dictionaries of the Hebrew and Greek Words by James Strong, MacDonald Publishing company, McLean, Virginia.

For our purpose, joy is defined as a composite of the Biblical definitions:

> Joy: 1. A deep inner hope that despite the circumstances my God will in time bring goodness and even cheer to my life again that He might proclaim His victory in me. 2. A calm sense of well-being based on our trust and dependence on him and from His divine influence upon my heart. 3. Gladness, a feeling of gratitude, satisfied gratification, and pleasure as we reflect on the thank-worthy moments of our life.

Horatio Spafford wrote the old hymn, "It Is Well with My Soul" in 1873, after having lost four daughters on an ocean voyage. Despite tremendous sorrow, he found "a calm sense of well-being based through his trust and dependence on God." In his own words, "When peace, like a river, attendeth my way, when sorrows like sea billows roll; Whatever my lot, thou has taught me to say, it is well, it is well, with my soul."

> Lift your eyes to the hills, sisters, and absorb the majesty of the Lord. Do you hear the mountains singing? As we watch the sunrise, shall we lift our hands and sing praises to the Almighty, Maker of heaven and earth? What a way to start our day!

Prayer: Lord, awaken our hearts to see, absorb, and be rejuvenated by your creation, the wild earth. Even decay in your system is a part of the nourishment and rebirth of life. Cultivate within each of us through your divine influence, a deep inner hope and a calm sense of well-being despite the circumstance. We surrender our brokenness to you. Amen.

Hide in My Heart: "I will sing of the mercies of the Lord forever; with my mouth will I make known, your faithfulness to all generations" (Psalm 89:1).

Choose Today: I chose to trust and hope in Him no matter my circumstances.

Week 9, Day 2. Read: Psalm 30.
Journal: What do you identify with most in David's song to God? How does David finish his psalm each time he pours out his sorrow? Ask your Father God to reveal the angst that keeps you from His peace.
Action Tool: to get outside to a park or wilderness area and go for a walk by yourself. Sing a song, lift your eyes to God's beauty and absorb little bits into your being. Notice light on the flowers, in the leaves, on the water. Look intently for details of loveliness. Receive His joy for those moments as a gift to you.

Week 9, Day 3. Read: Psalm 98:4-8.
Journal: What brings joy to your heart? Meditate on this and write what comes to mind.
Joy Trail: Choose Joy. How many days of your life do you want to waste being miserable? To find joy amid sorrow, you must set your mind to trusting God, choosing joy, looking for it, creating it.

Week 9, Day 4. Read: Philippians 4:4-13.
Journal: What beauty of God's creation brings you joy? What scenic view of nature speaks to you of serenity and peace?
Action Tool: Download and memorize a gospel song. Play it often until internalized.

Week 9, Day 5. Read: Nehemiah 8:8-12.
Journal: What can you celebrate today? Dwell on something small which brings joy. Journal your rejoicing.
Action Tool: Plan a mini celebration with some special food. It can be a cup of tea and a cookie for yourself or a dinner with friends. Just celebrate!

Pit of Self-Pity
Week 10, Day 1

> **This is the verdict: Light has come into the world, but men (women) loved darkness instead of light because their deeds were evil (thoughts were full of self-pity, etc.).**
>
> **(John 3:19)**

> It is a good thing, fellow pilgrims, we fortified ourselves with praise earlier this morning because we head into a dark cavernous pit today. Heft those packs and let's get going. Boy, did I say mine was fifty pounds when we started out? It weights one hundred now. Way too much for an old lady like me! I shouldn't have to do this anymore. Why couldn't God have supplied a pack mule for me? I deserve better than this. Why is it always me who must suffer?

One of my favorite sins and former past-times is self-pity. It is a very cozy sin, soothing and comforting, like a blankie. Besides, it doesn't hurt others not like alcoholism or fury or the other big ones. It is personal and private. Don't you agree? After all, it is unfair that my babies miscarried, my husband gets angry and my children are rebellious. Folks say, "Oh, you poor woman." Lots of Godly women unknowingly encourage feeling sorry for myself. No help needed, but nice to know this deep dark hole in the ground is "approved". I've papered it with scriptures, so I am sure God agrees.

Sometime along the way, my pity pit became large and well-appointed. It features a cushy reclining chair, lots of Kleenex, potato chips, chocolate bars plus consoling friends dropping by. Daily retreats to my pit gave me permission to wallow. In fact, an actual pain developed in my chest, heart palpitations, pulsing in my head, cramping in my stomach, dizziness. Sick and overwhelmed with tears, I did not bother to come out of this dark pit. God, I thought, did not care and my efforts were futile.

Does any of this terrain look familiar to you gals? It is steep and slippery going into the cavern. Yet, for some reason, we rush in, then complain about the damp and darkness. Wait, a minute! Do we really want to wallow in misery? Why did we go this way? Why not bypass this part of the journey? Here's how it happens, gals. Learn the signs to stop a slide into the pity-pit before you pick up speed.

The Way Down

- ❖ Something happens in your life that is unpleasant, irritating, painful or sorrowful.
- ❖ You compare your circumstances to someone who you think has it better than you.
- ❖ You dwell on the unfairness.
- ❖ You focus on bad circumstance and worry it will get much worse.
- ❖ You think, "Why me?" "I did nothing to deserve this."
- ❖ You curl into yourself, wallowing in the hurt, and misery.
- ❖ You comfort yourself with indulging in excesses of food, sleep, TV, cigarettes, drugs, shopping or another unhealthy compulsive habit.

Self-pity is a habit which perpetuates defeatist behavior. We will continue to dwell in misery extinguishing contentment even in the good moments if we allow self-pity to dominate our life. Self-pity is selfish self-love, all about me, with blindness to everyone else. Want a better life? Be ruthless with self-pity. Allow NO SELF-PITY, NO EXCUSES! We can always find a reason to feel sorry for ourselves. Self-pity has none, no not one, redemptive quality or constructive result. With the help of God, time to overcome this defeatist habit if you want to experience a victorious life.

The Way Up. Reaffirm…

- ❖ Life isn't fair for anyone!
- ❖ It is hard for everyone, even if I can't see their pain right now.
- ❖ God cares for me even if I do not feel it right now.

- ❖ God is working in me to conform me to the image of Christ.
- ❖ When I persevere through suffering, applying God's truth to my responses, God will refine me as pure gold.

> Girls, I see a light! Yes, come this way. Take the detour. God has provided a way of escape! Follow me but shoo away any pigs trailing after us.

Prayer: God of compassion, we do not know what to do with our sad, unhappy, lonely feelings so we hide in the dark pit of our own making. Self-pity cannot be defeated without your empowerment. We submit to your work within us no matter how hard. Help, Abba, help. Amen.
Hide in My Heart: "Praise the Lord, O my soul… who redeems your life from the pit and crowns you with love and compassion" (Psalm 103: 2a, 4)
Choose Today: I choose today to resist the devil and my own nature luring me into the pit.

Week 10, Day 2. Read: John 3:16-21.
Journal: Replace the word "evil" in today's verse with "thoughts of self-pity". By the way, self-pity is evil because it destroys our victory in Jesus. What circumstances trigger you to spiral downward? What are the repetitive hurts you do not deserve? Whom do you blame for your pain or depression? How do you comfort yourself? What do you say to yourself to justified self-pity?
Action Tool: Write on an index card (if you mean it), "As of today, self-pity is not an option. NO SELF PITY. NO EXCUSES!" Post this card on your bathroom mirror. Read it every morning.

Week 10, Day 3. Read: James 4:7 and Psalm 103:1-5.
Journal: Ask God to reveal how, with your unique make-up, to arise out of the pit. If you are unwilling to leave your well-appointed pity pit, pray that He will give you the willingness and the ability.

Action Tool: Using your "Eyes-Up" chart. Add a "Black Spot" each day you allow yourself to dwell in self-pity. Give yourself "Eyes Up with a smile" on the days you have victory against self-pity.

Week 10, Day 4. Read: Psalm 27:13-14.
Journal: What does "wait for the Lord" mean for you? How can you claim this scripture to be your own?
Action Tool: The Morning Rule. If you have fallen into the pity pit, in bed that night, tell yourself that in the morning, you will arise from the pit. Determine, no self-pity, no excuses through the power and strength of your God. Record on your Eyes-Up Chart a smile or black spot for yesterday.

Week 10, Day 5. Read: 2 Samuel 22:29 and Matthew 6:24-27.
Journal: Surrender your "sorry for yourself" reasons over to the Lord. Pray for your darkness to be transformed into light.
Action Tool: Record on your "Eyes Up" Chart a smile or black spot for yesterday.
Joy Trail: No Self-pity, no excuses. Even when we think we have a justified reason, self-pity is a slide into despair. Fill the void with a blessing.

Piggy Playpen at Swampy Lake
Week 11, Day 1

Like a gold ring in a pig's snout is a beautiful woman who shows no discretion.
(Proverbs 11:22)

> Sun, gorgeous sun, so bright on the eyes when we come out of the pit! Oh, my goodness, look at all those pigs. Hundreds, wallowing in the muddy shallows of Swampy Lake. Watch the little piglets' frolic and the big hogs laying there loving it. See the wild ones rooting for food with their noses while grunting away.

What do you think, girls? Laughter is one of God's fantastic gifts. Medical fact proves that laughter reduces pain and promotes healing. So, let's have fun while we lunch at Swampy Lake. ~

One of my husband's best qualities is his sense of humor and ability to make me laugh. In college, one of my favorite activities was watching little piglets in the agricultural unit. When our son was young, visiting the pigs became a favorite family outing. One morning years later, my husband told me there were pigs, cute little ones running around our kitchen. "Feeling-sorry-for-myself piglets" were oinking at him. Later, while walking by a lake, he named these selfish, self-loving pigs.

Excuse-to-be-Miserable Pigs

The Sad Sack Pig Family
<u>Passive Porker</u> – Papa Hog of the Sad Sack Family. "Uh, there's nothin' I can do about nothin'. Not worth trying. Just throw the slop down here. Grunt."

Pathetic Pig – Mama Sow of the Sad Sack Pig Family. "I am so pitiful; why would anything good come to me. Woe is me! Woe is me! I'll just lie here in the mud. Snort."

Poor Me Piglet – The cutest little piggy ever! "Life is just sooooo hard. May I have just one little, itty, bitty corn cob pleeeese?"

Petulant Piglet – "If I can't have it my way, I will just go hide in the muck and sulk. It's just not fair!"

Pandemonium Piglet – "Oh my goodness, the sky is falling! What will I do? What will I do?"

Packin' Pig – Uncle Pack is coated with dried on mud, thick and hard. "You don't understand...everything has gone against me all my life... rotten parents, bad marriage, miserable bosses. I'll get even, just you wait and see."

Persecuted Pig – Old Aunt Persecuted. "It's not my fault. I did nothin'. Everyone's against me; they just got it in fer me."

The Performance Pig Family

Postulating Pig – The Dominant hog of the Performance Pig Family. "Everyone's got it wrong. Can't they see? If they weren't so stupid, they would know my way is the right way. Why won't they listen?"

Perfection Pig – Mama Sow of the Performance Pig Family. "If you can't do it right, might as well not even get started. That's so not perfect! Oink."

Perhaps Piglet – This piglet is so adorable that everyone coddles her as she worries all day. "What if this happens? Or that? Or doesn't happen? Or could happen? Squeal."

Prissy Piglet – Little Prissy doesn't like to get her toes or snout dirty so she keeps out of the mud and muck. This makes it very hard to live in a swamp. "Why me? Why do I have to put up with all of this? It's not fair."

Procrastination Porker – Uncle Procrastination prefers to sit and watch. "Don't bug me. I'll get to it. Just as soon as I take a nap. Yes, but?"

Practical Pig – Big sister Practical Pig feels all the work of the family falls on her. "No one does anything around here except me. My life is just so hard. Whine, whine."

Any of these pigs familiar to you? Recognize your brother, sister, mom, dad, best friend? Recognize yourself? We all make excuses to feel sorry for ourselves at one time or another. Self-Pity is paralyzing. Do we really want to waste our lives lying around in a swamp of downer thinking? Rather,

> Apply your heart to instruction and your ears to words of knowledge. There is surely a future hope for you, and your hope will not be cut off.
>
> (Proverbs 23:12, 18)

> Why, my soul, are you downcast? Why so disturbed within me? Put your hope in God, for I will yet praise him, my Savior and my God.
>
> (Psalm 42:5)

We had fun with the pigs, didn't we? Not-so-fun, though, are self-destructive thought habits resulting in actions or inactions that defeat us. Once God convicted me of "no self-pity, no-excuses" a long journey began of catching my favorite "Poor Me" piglet and ousting it. Nowadays, the piglet family rarely visit. When they do, I shoo them out immediately. Well, maybe after one little bag of potato chips, I shoo them. Still working on it.

Prayer: Lord, we prefer to resist our nature and the evils one's lure to descend into the pit. But only through Your might and power is it possible. Today, we stand strong counting on you. Amen.
Hide in My Heart: "I call to God and the Lord saves me. As for me, I trust in you" (Psalm 55:16, 23b).
Choose Today: I choose to rely on the strength of God to resist and claim "No self-pity, no excuses".

Week 11, Day 2. Read: Psalm 42:5.
Journal: Identify your favorite pigs from the pig families. Record your triggers to indulge in of self-pity?

Action Tool:

- ❖ Get a big wide rubber band. Put it on your wrist.
- ❖ The moment a pig comes squealing into your life with words like "poor me, you never, this always, it's unfair, etc.", snap the rubber band so it stings your wrist.
- ❖ Look to Jesus, not the circumstance. Speak scripture out loud, Psalm 55:16.
- ❖ Do this for a week or a year until your pity pit is cemented shut. NO SELF-PITY, NO EXCUSES. SNAP OUT OF IT!

Week 11, Day 3. Scan Proverbs looking for scriptures that speak hope
Journal: Keep in mind your favorite "pigs". What scriptures counter your excuse to be miserable?
Action Tool: Continue to focus on NO SELF-PITY, NO EXCUSES. SNAP OUT OF IT! Record on your "Eyes Up" Chart a smile or black spot for yesterday.

Week 11, Day 4. Read: Psalm 55.
Journal: Journal what God has revealed to you for you from His word today.
Action Tool: Continue to focus on NO SELF-PITY, NO EXCUSES. SNAP OUT OF IT! Record on your "Eyes Up" Chart a smile or black spot for yesterday.

Week 11, Day 5. Read: Proverbs 23:12, 18.
Journal: How is your progress of applying your mind and heart to instruction?
Action Tool: Continue to focus on NO SELF-PITY, NO EXCUSES. SNAP OUT OF IT! Record on your "Eyes Up" Chart a smile or black spot for yesterday.

Pillars of Shame

Week 12, Day 1

> **Peace, I leave with you; my peace I give you. I do not give to your as the world gives. Do not let your hearts be troubled and do not be afraid.**
> **(John 14:27)**

> Trudge on, hikers, over the Pillars of Shame. These pillars of rock jut out of arid ground resembling stove pipes. Pipe upon pipe. Nothing but stunted bushes grow in this dry land. Yet God has important lessons to teach us while we walk this terrane, so keep your hearts open.

Our righteous God calls us to a higher standard than the world. He calls us to righteousness in the face of hate, chaos and evil. Yet, we are prone to embrace worldly behavior.

> There is no one righteous, not even one; there is no one who understands, no one who seeks God. All have turned away; they have together become worthless; there is no one who does good, not even one.
> (Romans 3:10–12)

In addition, we deceive ourselves:

> The heart is deceitful above all things and beyond cure. Who can understand it? I, the Lord, search the heart and examine the mind to reward a man according to his conduct, according to what his deeds deserve.
> (Jeremiah 17:9–10)

Let us drop in on Adam and Eve where it all started. God gave them everything, including free will and choice. They had it all, then they blew it.

Now the serpent was craftier than any of the wild animals the Lord God had made. He said to the woman, "Did God really say, 'You must not eat from any tree in the garden'?" The woman said to the serpent, "We may eat fruit from the trees in the garden, but God did say, 'You must not eat fruit from the tree that is in the middle of the garden, and you must not touch it, or you will die.'"

"You will not certainly die," the serpent said to the woman. "For God knows that when you eat from it your eyes will be opened, and you will be like God, knowing good and evil."

When the woman saw that the fruit of the tree was good for food and pleasing to the eye, and, desirable for gaining wisdom, she took some and ate it. She also gave some to her husband, who was with her, and he ate it. Then the eyes of both of them were opened, and they realized they were naked; so, they sewed fig leaves together and made coverings for themselves.

Then the man and his wife heard the sound of the Lord God as he was walking in the garden in the cool of the day, and they hid from the Lord God among the trees of the garden. But the Lord God called to the man, "Where are you?"

The man answered, "I heard you in the garden, and I was afraid because I was naked; so, I hid."

And the Lord God said, "Who told you that you were naked? Have you eaten from the tree that I commanded you not to eat from?"

The man said, "The woman you put here with me, she gave me some fruit from the tree, and I ate it."

Then the Lord God said to the woman, "What is this you have done?"

The woman said, "The serpent deceived me, and I ate."
(Genesis 3:3–13)

What happened in this momentous moment?

- Adam and Eve believed the half-truths of Satan: Know good and evil (true), not die (false), be like God (half-truth), God was keeping something good from them (false).
- They trusted the created (Satan) rather than the creator (God).
- Self-love wanted what it "perceived" was withheld. (Covetousness).
- Adam was not protecting his wife (care for the creation was Adam's job).
- Eve became the temptress seducing her husband to sin (rather than his help mate).
- Adam (who was with her) followed Eve and the serpent instead of God.
- They both chose disobedience (sin entered creation).

Results:

- They lost innocence. They became aware of good and evil (like God).
- They did not gain the wisdom of God (unlike God).
- Death entered in the form of shame, fear, blaming, enmity, and physical death. (as God said).
- Shame caused them to cover and hide (a form of death).
- The man blamed the woman and God (Not my fault, it was your fault!).
- The woman blamed the serpent. (It was his fault.)
- Harmony between husband and wife became a battle of egos (My way is right/best).

And so, the sin nature of mankind entered paradise. Thenceforth, we make excuses for our bad behaviors, naming them as "not sin" to justify our wrong doings. Not taking responsibility for our own actions, blaming others, or calling it habit or an addiction, or low self-esteem, we are free to say, "It's not my fault. I can't help it." Yet, God calls all of it sin. Choosing your own way instead of God's way is sin. The consequences are shame, guilt, fear, enmity and hardness of heart.

But God, who is rich in mercy, promises us a peace that surpasses all understanding, rest in Jesus and joy amid trials. He gives us the gift of gladness of heart. He has provided us with the fruit of the Holy Spirit to empower us to overcome our sin nature. Wow! (Based on John 14:22, 16:20, 33, Matthew 11:28, Ecclesiastes 5:18–20, Galatians 5:22–25)

> But the fruit of the Spirit is love, joy, peace, forbearance (patience), kindness, goodness, faithfulness, gentleness and self-control. Against such things there is no law. Those who belong to Christ Jesus have crucified the flesh with its passions and desires. Since we live by the Spirit, let us keep in step with the Spirit.
>
> (Galatians 5:22–25)

Yet, many of us think we were standing in the wrong line when this fruit was handed out. When we got to the counter they plunked, "Sold Out," in front of our face. So, we trudge along trying our best not to sin. Then something triggers us, and we fall into our favorite sinful habit, give up and sink back into the mire. "Oh, shame on you! You are so pitiful. You are worthless. Why should God give you joy or gladness or anything good when you can't even practice self-control for one day? You worm!"

Yep! We are guilty and undeserving of the fruit of the Spirit, every one of us. That is why monks in the 15th century developed self-flagellation (beating themselves with whips) hoping to purge themselves of their guilt and shame. Of course, it did not work, just gave them bloody backs. Yet, we self-flagellate when we beat ourselves with words of shame.

Perhaps, your parents verbally assaulted with "You, stupid kid. Can't you get anything right?" Now your inner voice gravitates to these phrases, repeating them incessantly. You say, "I suffer from low self-esteem." But that is not the issue. Each of us loves himself more than anyone else. Our selfishness guarantees we feed, indulge, and care for our self foremost. Yet, out of *sinful habit*, we self-flagellate. Some perverse reward motivates us to continue. Perhaps, our reward is attention, or a reason to indulge in habitual sin, false comfort, or an adrenaline high.

> Each one is tempted when, by his own evil desire, he is dragged away and enticed. Then, after desire has conceived, it gives birth to sin; and sin, when it is full grown, give birth to death.
>
> (James 1:14–15)

Remember also, that Satan is prowling around as a roaring lion waiting to attack you. (1 Peter 5:7–10) He cannot read your mind but sees your flaws. His dominions (evil spirits) are just waiting to whisper accusatory messages to destroy your joy in the Lord. Once you are Christ's, the devil cannot take your soul, so he determines to steal your joy and witness. If the devil (together with your own destructive habits) keeps you defeated, depressed, despairing, acting out and feeling worthless, of what good are you to spreading the love of Jesus?

We need a miracle… and God who is in the business of miracles gave us one. He gave us Jesus, our rescuer.

> But God demonstrates his own love for us in this: While we were still sinners, Christ died for us. Since we have now been justified by his blood, how much more shall we be saved from God's wrath through him! Not only is this so, but we also rejoice in God through our Lord Jesus Christ, through whom we have now received reconciliation.
>
> (Romans 5:8–9, 11)

God does not shame; that is the devil's work. God gives us a healthy conscience to warn us when we go astray and then offers repentance and forgiveness. Satan taunts us with never ending accusations, crippling us with shame. What is the cure? Do not retreat; attack! Claim your right as a child of God to His spiritual fruit. Tell the clerk at the spiritual fruit store you are a friend of the owner. He set aside a special box of fruit in the back room just for you. Remember,

> The fruit of the Spirit is love, joy, peace, patience, kindness, goodness, faithfulness, gentleness and SELF-CONTROL.

Since we live by the Spirit, let us keep in step with the Spirit.

(Galatians 5:22–23, 25)

These are not suggestions or goals, they are "gifts". Your job is to access whatever fruit you need through prayer moment by moment. Still, if you are like me, you forget and go it on your own strength once again. The antidote to strongholds of sin is applying God's truth. Therefore, when shame rears its ugly head:

- ❖ Don't listen, Stop It! Confess your weakness. (Psalm 61:2)
- ❖ Pray for Strength. (2 Corinthians 10:3–6)
- ❖ Repent and Turn Around. (Psalm 32:5)
- ❖ Healthy Comfort. (Philippians 3:14)
- ❖ Change your Thinking. (Romans 12:2)
- ❖ Rejoice. (Colossians 1:13–14)

God holds us accountable for our actions. We suffer the consequences of those actions. However, God is merciful and loving. Despite our failures, Jesus enables freedom from the power of sin. You can be a conqueror in Christ Jesus!

Oh, Sisters, what a long, long day. First the Pit of Self-Pity, Swampy Lake, then the Pillars of Shame. Oh no, it is drizzling. Quick, into the tent! We will fight off the gloom with song and scripture. "Oh, Lord, how majestic is thy name in all the earth…" Good night, Ladies.

Prayer: "Why are you downcast, O my soul? Why so disturbed within me? Put your hope in God for I will yet praise him, my Savior and my God. I call to God and the Lord saves me. Evening, morning and noon I cry out in distress, and he hears my voice. I cast my cares on the Lord and he will sustain me. When I am afraid, I will trust in you. In God, whose word I praise, in God I trust, I will not be afraid," (Psalm 42:11; 55:16–17, 22; 56:3–4). Amen.

Hide in My Heart: "In all these things, we are more than conquerors through him who loved us," (Romans 8:37).

Choose Today: I am forgiven. I am free. Victory over the cycle of shame is mine through Christ Jesus.

Week 12, Day 2. Read: Psalms 61:2, James 1:14–15 and Jeremiah 17:9–10.
Journal: Ask the Lord to reveal your personal downward path for a habitual sin or stronghold.
Action Tool: Don't listen, Stop It! Confess your weakness. Interrupt your emotional trigger or sinful thought with a sharp word, "Stop!", or shaking your hand hard or snapping a rubber band on your wrist. Select a signal to distract you from your thoughts. Practice this signal until it becomes routine.

Week 12, Day 3. Read: 2 Corinthians 10:3–6, Psalm 32:5, Hebrews 4:12 and Philippians 3:14.
Journal: Record a scripture to attack and win over your downward cycle?
Action Tool: Pray for strength. Repent and Turn Around. Memorize the "attack" scripture. Write it into your cell phone, write it on a card to tape on your bathroom mirror, another one to slip into your visor of your car. Keep the verse always at hand.

Week 12, Day 4. Read: Philippians 4:8 and Psalm 19.
Journal: With prayer write a list of healthy, beneficial thoughts and actions comforting to you. These should be short and quick to use as a replacement for your habitual sinful thoughts or actions. Put-off the sinful thought; Put-on the healthy thought. Put-off the sinful action; Put-on the healthy action.
Action Tool: Healthy Comfort. Choose one healthy thought and action as your "go to" when a trigger tempts you to spiral downward. Make a bracelet with "Pray" and the spiritual fruit you most need written in beads. Wear it daily.

Week 12, Day 5. Read: Romans 12:2, Romans 5:8–9, Colossians 1:13–14. **Action Tool: Change your Thinking. Rejoice.** Fill in your personal "Victory Plan" below. Write it on an index card to carry with you or post for easy viewing.

- ❖ GOD HELP! I own the power of self-control through Jesus Christ who strengthens me.
- ❖ STOP IT! My "Stop" signal_____.
- ❖ TURN AROUND. When I fail, I repent, ask forgiveness, and ACCEPT that forgiveness.
- ❖ HEALTHY COMFORT. I will comfort myself with this excellent thought "_____." and this excellent action, "_____.".
- ❖ MIND CHANGE. "I am more than a conqueror through him who loves me," (Romans 8:37).
- ❖ REJOICE. Say out loud, "I am forgiven. I am free. Victory is mine."

Valley of the Shadow of Death
Week 13, Day 1

> **My heart pounds, my strength fails me; even the light has gone from my eyes. O Lord do not forsake me; be not far from me, O my God. Come quickly to help me, O Lord my Savior.**
>
> **(Psalm 38:10, 21–22)**

> Pack up your wet tents, ladies; we continue today through a cold sunless valley. Even so, the sun is shining somewhere above the rain clouds. Besides we are more than conquerors through Christ Jesus! Though darkness may pierce our soul, Jesus is the light of the world and we claim light as our own. March on.

One beautiful sunny day, about forty years ago, some girlfriends and I were at the seashore seated behind large rocks eight feet above quiet surf. Preoccupied with laughing and chatting, we noticed no variation in the waves. Suddenly, a monster wave drenched us to our skin. Thank God, we were behind the rocks or we could have been swept out to sea. Tragedy is like that sudden wave, unexpected, overwhelming, out of our control, drenching us with a deep grief. There is no avoiding the grief; no pat answer or easy scripture that will be an antidote. We must walk through the darkness of grief until the light shines for us again. The feelings of anger, wanting to die, and absence of enjoyment is normal. If you've been there, you understand. All the "comforting words" others say are no comfort. Sorrow is a constant companion.

Sometimes our pain is so intense, our grief so real, we cannot see beyond our suffering. Once my deep grief and self-flagellation and anger at God made me so sick, I could not get off the couch all day. My grown son spoke lovingly, "Mom, stop dying and start living again." Those words motivated my return to life. I was killing myself emotionally, resulting in many physical ailments.

Deep grief can occur for many reasons. It results from death, be it the death of a family member, a relationship, a dream, health, finances, or your way of life. Grief goes through the process of disbelief, negotiation, anger, depression, then recuperation. Time must pass to process your emotions at each stage of grief; there are no short cuts. Tears must be shed. There is no easy way past the Valley of the Shadow of Death except *through* the grief. Still God walks through it with you.

> Even though I walk through the darkest valley, I will fear no evil, for you are with me; your rod and your staff, they comfort me.
>
> (Psalm 23:4)

At some point, to be whole again, you must choose life instead of death, peace and forgiveness instead of bitterness. You must decide to lean on God and allow him to lift you up. The time arrives when the season of grief needs to close. A time to feel joy again despite the sorrow.

> There is a time for everything, and a season for every activity under the heavens. A time to weep and a time to laugh, a time to mourn and a time to dance.
>
> (Ecclesiastes 3:1, 4)

Time to claim God's promise.

> I will give you a new heart and put a new spirit in you; I will remove from you your heart of stone and give you a heart of flesh.
>
> (Ezekiel 36:26)

When that time comes you must be tough on yourself.

> Get up, take up your mat and walk.
>
> (Mark 2:9b)

About all I could manage from my couch was "Help me God; give me a new heart." The next day I wobbled down the street (because of vertigo and illness). I got up and walked. It was a start.

> I know you are weary of trudging through these dark valleys, dear friends, yet we must continue on for another day. We will be of no value to ourselves, nor to the sisters in need of comfort, if we do not learn the lessons God teaches through suffering. Let's rest awhile beside this river and have a good cry.

Prayer: O Lord, as we wander in the dark valley, surround us with your peace that surpasses all understanding despite the sorrow we are suffering. Enable us to go through this deep grief without becoming bitter of heart. We so desperately need your presence to get us through. Amen.
Hide in My Heart: "I am still confident of this; I will see the goodness of the Lord in the land of the living. Wait for the Lord; be strong and take heart and wait for the Lord," (Psalm 27:13–14).
Choose Today: I will walk through this grief with you my God. I am not alone.

Week 13, Day 2. Read: Psalm 38:10, 21-22.
Journal: Pour out your heartbreak, bitterness, feelings of abandonment and questions of why to God. Take the time. Vent your pain on Him rather than dumping it on those who love you.
Joy Trail: Journal your pain.

Week 13, Day 3. Read: Psalms 69.
Journal: In what ways do you identify with King David's pain? How might you also claim his hope?
Action Tool: Write the memory verse (Hide in my Heart) on an index card. Set it beside your bed. Read it when you wake and retire until it raddles in your head.

Week 13, Day 4. Read: Ezekiel 36:26.
Journal: If you have huge insurmountable grief, pray for insights into how to face today. Ask for practical steps that will work for you. Record His insights.
Action Tool: Hug and pet a dog or cat. Ask a loved one for four bear hugs today. "I need a hug."

Week 13, Day 5. Read: Mark 2:1–12.
Journal: Laying paralyzed by our grief, we are in no shape to function. The paralyzed man could have said, "I can't," and continued to lay there. Instead he got up and walked home. How are you paralyzed? What is the first step for you to get up despite your grief?
Action Tool: Buy the book, Tear Soup: A Recipe for Healing after Loss by Pat Schiefer. This is a picture book suitable for women and children. It is a wonderful book showing the process of grief in a simple comforting story.

Crying River
Week 14, Day 1

> **There is a time for everything and a season for every activity under heaven: A time to weep and a time to laugh, a time to mourn and a time to dance.**
> **(Ecclesiastics 3:1, 4)**

> Wild and strong, the Crying River twists and turns, rocks hidden beneath the surface. For a while, drifting in your raft, warm sun, calm and quiet water restore peace to your fragmented mind. Suddenly, rapids swamp the raft flipping you into the swirling waters. Swept downstream, your lifejacket barely keeps you above the drowning waves. All you can do is keep your feet facing forward, gasp for air, and go with the flow of water until cast into an eddy. Hopefully, the following raft can rescue you.

Oh boy, I have been there, dear ones, both on an actual river and in my emotions. As we sit beside the river today, allow yourself to grieve. Shed those bottled-up tears. Give it to God and let go.

It is midnight in the hospital. I am wandering the halls in a daze when a nurse stops me, "Mrs. Del Vecchio, why did they move your husband from intensive care to pediatrics?" From a stupor, I mumble, "That isn't my husband in pediatrics; he is still in intensive care. That's my son."

"Oh, poor woman," she cried giving me a hug.

My husband was in the hospital near death with pneumonia. They opened his chest to scrape infection from the plural lining that day. On a short trip to my mom's earlier that evening to check on the children, I found my son throwing up, is lips blue, and his breathing shallow. At the hospital emergency room, they confirmed he had Hong Kong flu, combined with a serious asthma attack. The Hong Kong flu epidemic was in full swing with people dying. They admitted my son. I was so numb, I couldn't even cry. Now I was at risk of losing both my husband and son.

Sometimes, joy and peace are lost. The only prayer we can mutter is, "Help!" And that is enough. Cling to Jesus and hang on! He knows our every thought. He hears our heart crying out even when we do not have words to describe our anxious, hurt beyond hurt, pain and sorrow. At this point, we can turn bitter, ask why, struggle against God for allowing this in our life, or we can cling to the author of the universe. Just hang on despite the pain. And cry! A Godly woman once told me, "If a woman doesn't cry, she becomes hard."

> Out of the depths, I cry to you, O Lord; O Lord, hear my voice. Let your ears be attentive to my cry for mercy. .... I wait for the Lord, my soul waits, and in his word, I put my hope. My soul waits for the Lord more than watchmen wait for the morning, more than watchmen wait for the morning.
>
> (Psalms 130:1, 5)

In those times of great anguish, one cannot sleep at night due to fear and struggling. Physical aches or other symptoms may occur because of the great stress of grief. Allow yourself to cry healing tears, even bitter tears, even self-pity tears. Get alone and wail or call a close relative or friend and pour out your heart and tears to them. A little thing may trigger the tears. Let them flow. Give each tear to God our Father as a supplication. Hang on to Jesus with all your heart, for in due time, this season of weeping will pass.

> Do not fear, for I am with you; do not be dismayed, for I am your God. I will strengthen you and help you; I will uphold you with my righteous right hand.
>
> (Isaiah 41:10)

Each time the weeping is over, lift your head, wash your face, and take one step towards forgiveness, toward wholeness, towards joy. Focus on, the next right step. Ask God to reveal the next right step for you.

My husband and son both survived. I sailed through the near loss of my boy and husband with nary a tear or surface emotion. The toil those stuffed in emotions took on my body was serious. When they were both better, my days felt as if I were walking through mud, barely able to function. I was irritable and angry with those I loved. The doctor called it post-traumatic stress syndrome. Then one day, I cried and cried, afterwards slept. God's healing balm restored my health. Once again,

> You turned my wailing into dancing, you removed my sackcloth and clothed me with joy, that my heart may sing to you and not be silent. O lord my God, I will give you thanks forever.
>
> (Psalm 30:11)

Ok, Ladies, rinse out your handkerchief and tie it on your pack to dry. Crying time is over. Take the next step up and over the mountain. Put your boots on, pick up your walking stick, and on we trudge. Anyone for a chocolate raisin?

Prayer: Lord, some of us will not allow our self to cry. Some of us wallow in tears that never bring healing. Often, we are unable or unwilling to give our weeping to you and take the next step. Sometimes, we see no reason to get up off the couch and choose life. Lord, we ask you to take our time of sorrow, flood it with healing tears and bring good out of it. Perhaps, we will never dance again, Father, but at least tell us how to stand up and walk. Amen.

Hide in My Heart: "Do not fear, for I am with you; do not be dismayed, for I am your God. I will strengthen you and help you; I will uphold you with my righteous right hand, (Isaiah 41:10)."

Choose Today: I give my tears to you, Lord, and let go.

Week 14, Day 2. Read: Ecclesiastics 3:1–9.

Journal: Ask God to trigger healing tears you need to release. Give yourself permission to cry.

Joy Trail: Grieve deeply. Cry, wail, run, and talk to a friend or counselor. Then claim a scripture for restoring life to your soul and step out of misery.

Week 14, Day 3. Read: Psalms 130:1–5.
Journal: Do you have tapes in your heart telling you not to cry? If so, to whose voice are you listening? Are your tears manipulative or true grief? Do you feel better after tears or worse? Do you pray as you cry?
Action Tool: Continue walking every day. Listen to praise songs as you walk or take a friend that is quietly encouraging. Just go walking.

Week 14, Day 4. Read: Psalm 30.
Journal: At the end of each crying session, what words of affirmation do you need to hear? What words do you need to ingest or speak out loud to receive hope?
Action Tool: Drink plenty of water. Get the sleep you need. Dance around the room, whether or not you are in the mood.

Week 14, Day 5. Read: Isaiah 41:10.
Journal: Review the seasons of your life; seasons of laughter, seasons of weeping, seasons of mourning, seasons of dancing. Note these in your journal. How does it help to look at a time of crying as a season in your life?
Action Tool: Walk!

His Staff
Week 15, Day 1

> **I will fear no evil, for you are with me; your rod and your staff, they comfort me.**
> **(Psalm 23:4b)**

> Our walking sticks, gals, power and stabilize us on rough terrain. The staff of a shepherd protects and guides his sheep and herding dogs. The crooked neck aids in picking up lost, wounded or wayward lambs. He would wrap an injured lamb around his neck, carrying it on his shoulders until it healed. Jesus is our shepherd. Will we let Him carry us through these valleys?

The Lord allows us to experience the hardships of life just like everyone else on the planet. Sometimes he rescues us out of the situation, sometimes he does not. None the less, he promises to give us power and strength to endure in the midst, be comforted and become a better person on the other side of the pain. There is no "happy" in deep grief. The plan here is to hang onto God with all your might until the process of healing has matured sufficiently to feel life once more.

God sustained me during the dark night of my soul with these admonitions.

Arise and Come Forth Out of Grief:

- ❖ Read and reread psalms to be comforted by David's anguish and faith.
- ❖ Journal your angst like David in Psalm 6. After purging your hurt, declare "I will put my hope in God for I will yet praise him." Repeat daily as needed.

- Get alone, cry and wail; a solitary beach or woods is a great place, or even home alone.
- Walk, walk and walk some more. Physical exercise releases serotonin which lifts your spirit.
- Play uplifting, soothing music at home, in the car and while walking.
- Cry out, "God, help me make sense of this. God, help me survive. God, help me find joy again. God, help me get through today. God, help!"
- Read scripturally based Christian books on the grief process.
- Ask for hugs often.
- Soak in a hot tub. Get a massage. This releases the toxins emotions collected in your body.
- Volunteer to serve in a soup kitchen, children's ministry, visiting the elderly. Step outside of yourself.
- Affirm that you will get through this, "I can do all things through Christ who strengthens me. The sun will rise for me again one day."
- Decide that "Just for Today", I will concentrate on a positive action rather than on my grief.
- Read or recite the 23rd Psalm every night when you lay your head on your pillow.
- Find support from a friend whose company brings a sense of peace.
- Seek an organized Christian support group for grief recovery.

Bad things happen because we live in a fallen, corrupt world. Some grief will last a lifetime and never be totally healed. We do not understand and cannot accept that it happened to us. Yet it has happened, so we now have a choice. Be bitter and go it alone or cling to God who will somehow, though it seems impossible, work this together for good and bring life out of this valley of the shadow of death.

> Some folks cling to the darkness, dear wounded friends, yet we are seeking light. That is the purpose of this journey. Before Jesus raised Lazarus from the dead, spectators exclaimed, "He stinketh". Pain and grief "stinketh" but Jesus will raise you from this death if you follow his bidding to "arise and come forth".
>
> (John 11:38)

Prayer: "Be merciful to me, O Lord, for I am in distress; my eyes grow weak with sorrow, my soul and my body with grief. My life is consumed by anguish and my years by groaning; my strength fails because of my affliction and my bones grow weak. But I trust in you, O Lord; I say, "You are my God. My times are in your hands. Let your face shine on your servant; save me in your unfailing love," (Psalm 31:9-10, 14,16).
Hide in My Heart: The 23rd Psalm.
Choose Today: I choose the path to light one step at a time as God leads.

Week 15, Day 2. Read Psalm 23 slowly. Absorb comfort.
Journal: In what ways do you "hang on" to God in times of grief? What are some new ways God is guiding you to get through this season?
Action Tool: Signify giving your sorrow over to God by lifting your closed hands to the sky, then open your hands letting go of this pain to your Lord and Savior. Recite often during the day, "He restores my soul."

Week 15, Day 3. Read: Matthew 26:36-52; 27:45-50; Luke 22:41-44.
Journal: How is your grief similar to the grief Jesus felt? Have loved ones betrayed you? Do you feel forsaken by God? Do you believe that God the Father will raise you up again?
Action Tool: Affirm every day that you will get through this "I can do all things through Christ who strengthens me. The sun will rise for me one day. I will wait upon His healing touch."

Week 15, Day 4. Read: John 11:1-45 The story of Lazarus
Journal: Write Psalm 31: 9-10, 14,16 into your journal as a personal prayer.
Action Tool: Plan to take the next right step. Review the lesson list for ideas.

Week 1,5 Day 5. Read: Psalm 121.
Journal: Even though hardships continue in our lifetime on this earth, how does Psalm 121 speak to your heart of God's constant presence in your life?
Joy Trail: Take a mental vacation. Is there a place that made your spirit soar? Breathe slowly in and out and think of that place for a few moments. Post pictures of this place in your home.

Expectation Pass
Week 16, Day 1

> **For I know the plans I have for you," declares the Lord, "plans to prosper you and not to harm you, plans to give you hope and a future.**
>
> **(Jeremiah 29:11)**

> Eyes up, ladies, our route today takes us through Expectation Pass, past Acceptance Grotto, to the Hills of Hope. About time! It is so exhausting walking in the dark and shadows. Don your packs, gals, and lift your face to the sunshine!

Oh, that we had a magic wand and could wave away doubts, fears, trouble, pain and sorrow. Yes, let's do it! Then we will be happy, happy, happy! Well, God could do it but most often he does not. Why? Because he gave human beings free will. Having free will means choice. We can choose good or evil, righteousness or sin, healthy or unhealthy, emotional death or life. Every human is given choices, Christian or not. Their choices affect our family, neighbors, towns, country, and world. With people often choosing death over life, sin over righteousness, expect suffering.

Let's assume you and I decide on abundant life. We choose to believe despite our unbelief and to apply the word of God to our lives. What can we expect in daily life? Sorry to tell you, some bad news but also good news!

Bad News:

- ❖ Often, it will appear God does not hear our cries.
- ❖ Jesus will sometimes seem far away.
- ❖ Habits, strongholds, and grief are not easily overcome.

- ❖ God will not wave a magic wand.
- ❖ We will fail along the way.
- ❖ Others will hurt and disappoint us.

With this depressing reality why bother? Because…

> No temptation has seized you except what is common to man. And God is faithful; he will not let you be tempted beyond what you can bear. But when you are tempted, he will also provide a way out so that you can stand up under it.
>
> (1 Corinthians 10:13)

Good News:

- ❖ God is in the midst, *with us,* no matter what we feel.
- ❖ We are saved by grace, through faith, not by our works.
- ❖ He is working within us to will and to act.
- ❖ He will bring us joy and gladness of heart as we become more connected to him.
- ❖ As we yield to God, our grief, habits and sinful strongholds will be healed.
- ❖ Our God forgives our failures, if we but repent and look to Jesus once again.
- ❖ Our faith will give us hope in our daily circumstances even when they are hard.
- ❖ He hears. He cares; He is acting. Guaranteed! HALLELUIA!

Listen to our spiritual ancestors as they suffered deplorable reality. David being persecuted by Saul cried out,

> How long, O Lord? Will you forget me forever? How long will you hide your face from me? How long must I wrestle with my thoughts and every day have sorrow in my heart? Look on me and answer, O Lord my God. Give light to my eyes, or I will sleep in death. …But I trust in your

unfailing love; my heart rejoices in your salvation. I will sing to the Lord, for he has been good to me.

(Psalm 13:1–6)

Paul, locked in a prison wrote,

> Therefore, since we have been justified through faith, we have peace with God through our Lord Jesus Christ, through whom we have gained access by faith into this grace in which we now stand. And we rejoice in the hope of the glory of God. Not only so, but we also rejoice in our sufferings, because we know that suffering produces perseverance; perseverance, character; and character, hope. And hope does not disappoint us, because God has poured out his love into our hearts by the Holy Spirit, whom he has given us.
>
> (Romans 5:1–5)

John from exile wrote,

> How great is the love the Father has lavished on us that we should be called children of God! And that is what we are!
>
> (1 John 3:1)

This is what God says about us:

- ❖ He knows our name. (John 10:3)
- ❖ He numbers the hairs on our head. (Matt 10:30)
- ❖ He counts the steps of our feet. (Job 14:16)
- ❖ He holds our right hand in his hand. (Psalms 73:23)
- ❖ He supplies all our needs. (Philippians 11:19)

To bring it home, expect seeking joy and peace by applying His Word in practical ways will be a lifelong endeavor. Along the way you will falter or be smacked by circumstances, just make a U-turn, eyes up once again, and keep walking towards Jesus. Gladness of heart, contentment, joy, be it only for a moment or a deep within your soul, will be your reward. COUNT NOT ON MAN'S FAITHFULNESS BUT ON GOD'S.

> "And they lived happily ever-after. The End." We grew up on that, didn't we girls? We believed it and craved it. In her seventies, my Mama explained, "A marriage or life may *appear* perfect. We just cannot see the struggles and hard work behind closed doors. No one escapes." Our happily-ever-after life comes from years of walking with God through the hills and valleys. Facing this reality helps us move beyond our expectations to the serenity of acceptance.

Prayer: My Jesus, thank you for coming into my fallen world and giving me victory. Even though I experience tribulation, I will be of good cheer. Thank you, Jesus. Amen.

Hide in My Heart: "No temptation has seized you except what is common to man. And God is faithful; he will not let you be tempted beyond what you can bear. But when you are tempted, he will also provide a way out so that you can stand up under it," (1 Corinthians 10:13)

Choose Today: I choose to count not on man's faithfulness, but on God's faithfulness.

Week 16, Day 2. Read: 1 Corinthians 10:13.
Journal: When are your temptations unbearable? Ask God the way out so you can stand and not cave.
Action Tool: Write "Count not on man's faithfulness, but on God's faithfulness," on a card. Post it on your mirror.

Week 16, Day 3. Read: Romans 5:1–5.
Journal: Pour out your expectations and disappointments. How do your expectations differ from your reality? Pray for the ability to hope amid struggles. Become better not bitter.

Action Tool: Create a U-Turn signal to use when you wander onto the wrong path. Do a circle in the air with your finger or turn your body around and take a step in the opposite direction. Then close your hand and hold it to your heart as a sign of taking the hand of God.

Week 1,6 Day 4. Read the scripture verses from the lesson points, "This is what God says about us."
Journal: How has God shown His love for you amid disappointments? Pray for His comfort when needed. For wherever sin (sorrow) is plentiful His abundant grace abounds.
Action Tool: Sing a hymn in worship.

Week 16, Day 5. Read: Jeremiah 29:11 and Proverbs 15:30.
Journal: How has God been shaping your character? How have you grown in Godliness during this season? Though it may be a season of sorrow, describe a season of hope.
Joy Trail: Cultivate laughter. Laughter is healing. Believe it or not, healing occurs even when we fake laughter and smiling. Fake laugh alone in the car until it is real again.

Acceptance Grotto
Week 17, Day 1

> **And Mary said, "My soul glorifies the Lord and my spirit rejoices in God my Savior, for he has been mindful of the humble state of his servant, for the Mighty One has done great things for me, holy is his name."**
>
> **(Luke 1:46–49)**

> Step aside, sisters, into the Acceptance Grotto. If we are fortunate, Mother Mary waits for us. Mary epitomizes acceptance. As a teen, she was overshadowed by the Holy Spirit and conceived the Son of God. Her response was, "I am the Lord's servant. May it be to me as you have said," (Luke 1:38). Life wasn't easy for her. Even Joseph didn't believe her. Would you? Do you? Her baby was born around animal dung. They fled to escape the slaughter of baby boys. She watched her son crucified. This was her reality. Even so, she said, "My spirit rejoices in God my Savior." Let us sit awhile in the cool grotto and contemplate acceptance.

A friend's email states, "lifeslikethat". Wish that it was not "like that", but it is. My daughter says, "It is what it is." This little phrase helps when one cannot change the circumstance. For peace, we must find acceptance. Focus for a moment on the "Serenity Prayer" of St. Francis of Assisi:

> God grant me the serenity
> To accept the things I cannot change,
> Courage to change the things I can,
> And wisdom to know the difference.

Read again, "accept the things I cannot change." Accept that marriage may not be as we imagined. Accept miscarriages. Accept a downs syndrome child. Accept singleness. Accept a lost job resulting in a foreclosed house. Accept a death. Long is the list. We do not want to accept these things. We want to fight against them. "It's not FAIR!" Well, life is not fair. Life is HARD.

> I have told you these things, so that in me you may have peace. In this world you will have trouble. But take heart! I have overcome the world.
>
> (John 16:33)

And being God's child, we are called,

> To take up our cross daily and follow him.
>
> (Luke 9:23)

Consider the phrase, "Courage to change the things I can, and wisdom to know the difference." Ultimately, we can change no-one but ourselves and it takes much courage, prayer and perseverance to do so. We must ask God for wisdom regarding what to change and when to accept.

> Consider it pure joy, my sisters, whenever you face trials of many kinds, because you know that the testing of your faith develops perseverance. Perseverance must finish its work so that you may be mature and complete, not lacking anything. If any of you lacks wisdom, he should ask God, who gives generously to all without finding fault, and it will be given to her.
>
> (James 1: 2)

God promises it will be worthwhile in the end. Having shared with you my struggles, realize blessings are abundant in my life as well. My toil over the years of depending on the Lord, brought worthwhile results. I rejoice in amazement, given our tumultuous years, at the present miraculous sweetness with my husband, son and daughter!

> Blessed is the man (woman) who perseveres under trial, because when she has stood the test, he will receive the crown of life that God has promised to those who love him.
>
> (James 1:12)

Posted on the wall of the orphanage founded by Mother Teresa of Calcutta was a modified version of a poem, Paradoxical Commandments, written by Dr. Kent Keith. Notice how it encourages us to accept life and yet persist in goodness anyway.

ANYWAY

People are unreasonable, illogical, and self-centered,
LOVE THEM ANYWAY
If you do good, people will accuse you of
selfish, ulterior motives,
DO GOOD ANYWAY
If you are successful,
you win false friends and true enemies,
SUCCEED ANYWAY
The good you do will be forgotten tomorrow,
DO GOOD ANYWAY
Honesty and frankness make you vulnerable,
BE HONEST AND FRANK ANYWAY
What you spent years building may be
destroyed overnight,
BUILD ANYWAY
People really need help
but may attack you if you help them,
HELP PEOPLE ANYWAY
Give the world the best you have
And you'll get kicked in the teeth,
GIVE THE WORLD THE BEST YOU'VE GOT ANYWAY.

Reported in <u>Mother Teresa: A Simple Path,</u> compiled by Lucinda Vardey (New York: Ballantine Books, 1995), page 185. Vardey said it was "A sign on the wall of Shishu Bhavan, the children's home in Calcutta."

"Accepting things I cannot change, while working to change the things I can," enables us to be and do our best.

> Dear friends do not be surprised at the painful trial you are suffering, as though something strange were happening to you. But rejoice that you participate in the sufferings of Christ so that you may be overjoyed when his glory is revealed.
>
> (1 Peter 4:12)

If we spend our energy on denying, refuting, and grumbling about the things we cannot change, we exhaust strength better used to change the things we can. Acceptance of trials is a beginning, wisdom and courage to make a difference is our prayer.

> Such encouragement, sitting quietly with Mary in the Acceptance Grotto. God is good. Look ahead, girls; we can see the Hills of Hope up yonder. Can't wait to get there. Let's sing while we walk, "Onward Christian soldiers, marching as to God. With the cross of Jesus going on before.".

Prayer: Lord, give us strong hearts, willing and ready to forgive and be kind "anyway". We pray for your wisdom regarding acceptance and changes needed. Guide us, Father, for we are weak. Thank you for walking with us. In Jesus name, Amen.

Hide in My Heart: "I have told you these things, so that in me you may have peace. In this world you will have trouble. But take heart! I have overcome the world," (John 16:33).

Choose Today: I will give the world the best I have. It may never be enough. I choose to give the world my best anyway.

Week 17, Day 2. Read: John 16:33 and 1 Peter 4:12.
Journal: What circumstances are you ineffectively fighting? Your singleness? Your husband or children's behaviors? Work? Health? State of the world? What can you change and what is out of your control?
Joy Trail: Accept Reality. Look realistically at your circumstance. Consider what you can and cannot do to change it. Take the action you can, accept what you cannot change.

Week 17, Day 3. Read: Galatians 5.
Journal: Ask God to show you a significant issue in your life which you cannot change. What do you need to "accept"?
Action Tool: Who in your life is unreasonable, illogical and self-centered? Forgive them today through the power of God within you.

Week 17, Day 4. Reread: Galatians 5: 22 Fruit of the spirit.
Journal: Pray for willingness, wisdom, power and persistence to deal with the issue from yesterday. Write an action list of changes needed.
Action Tool: Do a random act of kindness today. Ask the Lord to show you the moment and action needed, a God appointment for you today.

Week 17, Day 5. Read: James 1:12.
Journal: How can you persevere showing the world your Godly best "anyway"?
Action Tool: Send a note to someone today handwritten on stationary with the poem "Anyway". Be an encouragement to someone else and you will encourage yourself.

Hills of Hope
Week 18, Day 1

> **You will go out in joy and be led forth in peace; the mountains and hills will burst into song before you, and all the trees of the field will clap their hands.**
> **(Isaiah 55:12)**

> Bask in the sunlight, Ladies. Let the gentle breeze kiss your face as the Holy Spirit heals your thoughts here on the Hills of Hope. Allow the natural loveliness of the forest woodland to permeate your heart and soul. Soak in His love. God bestows gladness as a gift in ordinary life; accept this gift into your inner being. We shall camp here for a while.

As a young woman touring Europe, I attended the Lipizzaner Horses' performance in Austria. These magnificent white horses dance to classical music. Trainers raise these horses on rough, barren, wild ground to develop strength to perform. Colts raised in comfortable barn yards, I learned, do not have the stamina necessary.

It is the same with us; we become weak without testing and trials. These trials are our "rough and barren ground", where we learn to depend on God and respond with the fruits of the spirit. Think of how many wealthy movie stars descend into the pit despite their affluence and comfort. Even though God allows hardships to mold us, He shares many reasons to have Biblical hope and joy. We can have HOPE and seek JOY even in the most difficult of circumstances. As a reminder, here again is our definition of joy:

> Joy. 1: A deep inner hope that despite the circumstances my God will, in time, bring goodness and even cheer to my life again, that He might proclaim His victory

in me. 2: A calm sense of well-being based on our trust and dependence on him and from His divine influence upon my heart. 3: Gladness, feelings of gratitude, satisfied gratification, and pleasure as we reflect on the thank-worthy moments of our life.

Scriptural Reasons for Joy:

1. Joy for the word of God recorded for us in the Bible. (Psalm 19)
2. Joy from assurance of sins forgiven. (John 3:16)
3. The love of God for each one of us. (John 15:9–11)
4. Joy because of hope. (Psalm 30:11, Romans 15:13)
5. Faith and hope despite the circumstances. (Isaiah 40:31, Habakkuk 3:17–18)
6. Joy because we know goodness will come out of hardship (if we allow him to work in us) for those who love God. (Romans 8:28–30)
7. Joy because our character is being formed to be mature and complete. (James 1:2–4)
8. Joy for our confidence that Jesus can bring life out death. (2 Timothy 1:8–10)
9. Joy for the grace God has given to us. (2 Corinthians 9: 8)
10. God Himself is our strength. (Philippians 4:13)
11. God will meet our needs. (Philippians 4:19)
12. Joy in the Holy Spirit. (Romans 14:17, John 14: 26)
13. Joy in obedience to God. (John 15: 1-17)
14. For the fruit of the Spirit. (Galatians 5:22–23)
15. When children choose well. (Proverbs 10:1)
16. The birth of a child. (John 16:21)
17. For grandchildren. (Proverbs 17:6)
18. We are called children of God. (1 John 3:1)
19. Cheerful looks and words. (Proverbs 15:30)
20. For the strength He gives us. (Psalm 81:1, Psalm 28:7)
21. For the peace of God. (John 14:27)
22. That we may come into His presence. (Psalm 27:4–5)

23. For the gift of gladness of heart. (Ecclesiastes 5:18–20)
24. For satisfaction in our work, enjoyment of food and possessions. (Ecclesiastes 5:18–20)
25. Joy in nature for everything God created is good. (Genesis 1:31, Isaiah 55:12)
26. A good night's sleep. (Psalm 4:8)
27. For whatever is noble, right, pure, lovely, admirable, and excellent or praiseworthy. (Philippians 4:8–9)
28. For love in action. (1 Corinthians 13:4–8)
29. For the freedom to gather and sing praises to the Lord. (Psalm 100)
30. For His promises:

> Then maidens will dance and be glad, young men and old as well. I will turn their mourning into gladness; I will give them comfort and joy instead of sorrow.
> (Jeremiah 31:13)

Isn't it amazing, fellow pilgrims, that we can have any peace of mind or joy amid our troubled world and tumultuous lives? Only through our God is it possible because we have a God who takes part in our lives. Still struggling? Expected. Keep praying for God's gift of hope despite the circumstances. It will come. Listen to the hills singing! Shall we join in?

Prayer: "Open my eyes, Lord, I want to see Jesus. To reach out and touch Him and say that I love Him." Open my eyes, Lord, to see the joy you have placed before me and around me. In Jesus name, Amen.

Hide in My Heart: "May you, my God of hope fill me with all joy and peace as I trust in You, so I overflow with hope by the power of the Holy Spirit," (Romans 15:13).

Choose Today: "Though the fig tree does not bud… I will be joyful in God my Savior," (Habakkuk 3:17–18).

Week 18, Day 2. Read Scriptures from items 1-9.
Journal: Record a scripture significant to you from today's verses.
Action Tool: Today when someone says, "Hi, how are you?" say back to them with a smile, "Appreciative. Thank you. And you?" Even if you are grumpy, saying appreciative will remind you and uplift your spirits.

Week 18, Day 3. Read Scriptures from items 10–16.
Journal: What is good in your life? List 20 joys. Keep on praying and listing until you have at least 20.
Action Tool: Share your list on Facebook.

Week 18, Day 4. Read Scriptures from items 17-24.
Journal: Record scripture which jumped out at you.
Joy Trail: Focus on the moment. Notice something *right* this moment, that is soothing, lovely, darling, funny, relaxing, and good, comforting, loving. Then focus on it, savor it, absorb it for just this moment.

Week 18, Day 5. Read Scriptures from items 23-30.
Journal: What has God spoken to you this week?
Action Tool: Send a note to someone describing how they brought you joy. A handwritten note and scripture stamped and mailed speaks volumes about God's love for the recipient.

Stinging Nettles
Week 19, Day 1

No discipline seems pleasant at the time, but painful. Later on, however, it produces a harvest of righteousness and peace for those who have been trained by it.
(Hebrews 12:11)

> Girlfriends, shall we explore a bit on the Hills of Hope? I remember a glade over this way with a crystal spring bubbling out of the ground. We can fill our water bottles. Ouch! Watch it girls, nettles. I brushed against a nettle and got stung. Ohhhhh, it hurts!

Can you identify a stinging nettle? It is an herbaceous plant that has jagged leaves covered with stinging hairs. This plant has a vicious sting that last for hours. Why did God make this plant? I don't know, but I know why God made pain. It is a gift from God to aid us in healing. Pain is, well painful, yet also, a signal to inform us that something is wrong. A stinging nettle!

A red light blinking on the dashboard of your car is an indicator that something is wrong. Red lights at a street corner demands, "Stop". Pain is a red light, a stinging nettle, that God has installed into our system as a warning that something needs attention. Our pain is, in fact, a blessing.

Imagine if you did not feel pain when touching a heated oven. Your searing flesh would not instantly cause your hand to jerk away. An infection may fester, yet nothing motivates you to treat it. On the other hand, physical pain, even a small splinter, irritates so much we are relentless at seeking relief. Emotional pain is a large flashing red light and screaming siren, think 911. Something is wrong; we must stop and pay attention. It may be a splinter of irritation between you and a family member, or a screaming pain of loss. No matter the size, ignoring the pain will cause it to fester into bitterness. Pay attention to your emotional pain as a warning signal of changes needed.

A silly example of a stinging nettle in my home was a missing pencil. The pencil by the phone disappeared when my husband needed it (this was when phones attached to a wall). He reacted upset and frustrated. I would go l looking for one, myself now irritated. Finally, paying attention to this irritant, a box of pencil was bought and sharpened. When they disappeared, I bought another. A simple solution to a small irritant. Duh! If you have a splintered relationship or broken heart, pay attention to the warning light. Pain of any kind must become a signal for you to pray. Ask the Lord to guide you into healing, to give you creative solutions, forgiveness, strength and courage.

The desire to change must exceed the pain of staying the same. Seek God first, his wisdom and direction in scripture. Seek Bible based counsel from Godly people. For daily irritations, examine the cause and pray for a solution. You cannot change someone else, only yourself. What can you do, with God's help, to be stronger, make changes, and be hopeful and find peace in the situation?

> Humble yourselves, therefore, under God's mighty hand, that he may lift you up in due time. Cast all your anxiety on him because he cares for you. Be self-controlled and alert. Your enemy the devil prowls around like a roaring lion looking for someone to devour. Resist him, standing firm in the faith, because you know that your brothers (sisters) throughout the world are undergoing the same kind of sufferings. And the God of all grace, who called you to his eternal glory in Christ, after you have suffered a little while, will himself restore you and make you strong, firm and steadfast. To him be the power forever. Amen.
>
> (1 Peter 5:6–11)

> Oh, my goodness, the nettles are still stinging, ouch…! Ok, gotta' treat it. A little dirt and spit to make mud applied to the sting will help remove the nettles. Or adhesive tape or a dock plant. This plant often grows conveniently around nettles. God is so practical. If I rub the leaves of the dock plant on the nettle sting, the pain should subside.

Prayer: Lord, you tell us to be thankful in (not because of) all circumstances. It is so hard to be thankful for pain, yet we understand that even pain is a gift from you, a warning that something is wrong. Help us grasp what action is needed in our painful circumstances. Have mercy upon us, O Father God, and restore each one of us to wholeness. Amen.
Hide in My Heart: "Humble yourselves, therefore, under God's mighty hand, that he may lift you up in due time. Cast all your anxiety on him because he cares for you" (1 Peter 5:6–7).
Choose Today: I choose to look at pain as a blessing because it alerts me to something that is wrong and needs attention.

Week 19, Day 2. Read: 1 Peter 5:8–9.
Journal: How might the devil be trying to devour you? What lies are you hearing? Lift these concerns to God in prayer.
Action Tool: Declare out loud (because the devil cannot read your thoughts), "Through the power of Jesus, I will not listen to your lies, evil one. I stand with Jesus my savior and will follow His voice only."

Week 19, Day 3. Read: 1 Peter 5:10–11.
Journal: If your pain is screaming you are well-aware of it. What is this pain speaking to you? What is wrong that needs attention in your life? Pray for a God guided salve.
Action Tool: When pain strikes, think 911, Emergency! Call Jesus!

Week 19, Day 4. Read: 1 Peter 5:6–7.
Action Tool: Try an exercise in nettle removal.

- Sit quietly alone with the Lord, eyes closed.
- Breathe in slow and deep, and then exhale slowly.
- As you breathe in, affirm to God, "I trust in you." As you exhale, affirm, "I am resting in Jesus."
- Lift your hands to your head. Slowly raise your hands lifting your hair.
- Visualize each strand of hair as a stress, sorrow, pain. Symbolically draw stress out of your head.
- Now, with your hands in the air, throw your cares upon Jesus. Visualize Jesus catching the cares where they burn away in the fire of His love.
- Tell your God, "Not my will but thy will be done."
- Take a few deeper breaths affirming, "I trust in you," and "I am resting in Jesus."
- Sit still and rest.

Week 19, Day 5. Read: Hebrews 12:1–12.
Journal: How do your "stinging nettles" indicate a way to "strengthen your feeble arms and weak knees" so you will not "grow weary and lose heart"? Rest in Jesus until He reveals a way to you.
Action Tool: Irritated? Think "Stinging Nettle". Look for an antidote nearby.

Sunlit Glade
Week 20, Day 1

> **If anyone loves me, he will obey my teaching. My Father will love him, and we will come to him and make our home with him. He who does not love me will not obey my teaching. These words you hear are not my own; they belong to the Father who sent me.**
> **(John 14:23–24)**

> Thank goodness, the stinging from the nettles has stopped. Come gals, over here to this lovely little glade. Here on the Hills of Hope tiny alpine wildflowers dot the grass and a clear spring bubbles from deep in the ground. Just imagine fairies dancing in the filtered sunlight. Sunlit Glade is a place of respite, a treasure of delight as we journey over the Mountain of Gloom in obedience to our Lord.

Jesus says, "If you love me, you will obey me."
(John 14:23)

Love motivates obedience. Prior to being adopted at age three and a half, my daughter lived confined to a crib in a Romanian orphanage. The orphanage housed one hundred twenty-five toddlers with three adults to care for them. Workers propped bottles against a blanket, rarely talked to or held a child except for diaper changing. They herded the toddlers like cattle with switches. The survivors learned to comfort themselves by rocking or crying for long hours. Many children died. When I brought Monica home, she saw no reason to obey me. Love was not an emotion she ever experienced receiving or giving. She had no conscience regarding right or wrong.

Babies learn from the moment of birth about love as their mothers and fathers coo at them and nuzzle their neck with kisses. Toddlers in a family are well-aware of "I love you" and "No, no". Love and discipline. They are also well-aware that parents provide nourishment, warmth and protection. Depending on the child's temperament, it motivates them to obey in order to get something they want such as food, toys, cuddling. My daughter had learned that her actions did not result in blessings. No one responded to her. In fact, destructive behaviors drew attention in the orphanage so were repeated in her new home. Over much time, she experienced love and steadfastness, creating the ability to love back. This gave her a reason to obey the values of family and society resulting in multiple blessings.

In the same way that a parent loves her baby, before the baby even understands love, our Heavenly Father loves us.

> And so, we know and rely on the love God has for us. God is love. Whoever lives in love lives in God and God in him. We love because he first loved us.
>
> (John 4:16, 19)

Learning to love our God and Savior is crucial to our willingness to obey Him. To experience His love, we must be in relationship with Him through the word, prayer, and fellowship. As He works in our life, we internalize that *obedience to God brings blessings, disobedience brings consequences.*

Jesus, in his own words, makes this clear.

Obedience: "I have set an example that you should do as I have done for you," (John 13:15).
Blessing: "Now that you know these things, you will be blessed if you do them," (John 13:17).
Obedience: "If you love me, you will obey what I command," (John 14:15).
Blessing: "And I will ask the Father, and he will give you another Counselor to be with you forever, the Spirit of truth," (John 14: 16).
Obedience: "Whoever has my commands and obeys them, he is the one who loves me," (John 14:21a).

Blessing: "He who loves me will be loved by my Father, and I too will love him and show myself to him," (John 14:21b).
Obedience: "Now remain in my love. If you obey my commands, you will remain in my love, just as I have obeyed my Father's commands and remain in his love," (John 15:9-10).
Blessing: "I have told you this so that my joy may be in you and that your joy may be complete," (John 15:11).

Given these promises, we should naturally obey our Lord. However, our human temperament brings additional stumbling blocks to obedience. Little Johnny wants cookies! Chocolate chip cookies, for breakfast, lunch and dinner. His mommy is clear, two cookies after lunch and two more after a healthy dinner. But Johnny has a plan. Pull a chair over, climb up on the counter, grab the bag of cookies and hide it under his bed. Oh, cookies all day; feeling yucky that night. Repeat this for a lifetime. Fast forward, John is grown, fat, unhealthy, often sick and struggling with fad diets. Obedience to his mom would have brought vitality and health yet the call of cookies was too strong.

Aren't we all little Johnny's? Each of us is called by some unhealthy physical, emotional, or spiritual attraction. The Bible is clear how to obey, yet the lure of our "cookie" is strong, so we opt for instant gratification. Later we suffer the long-term consequences.

> When tempted, no one should say, "God is tempting me." For God cannot be tempted by evil, nor does he tempt anyone; but each one is tempted when, by his own evil desire, he is dragged away and enticed. Then, after desire has conceived, it gives birth to sin; and sin, when it is full-grown, gives birth to death.
> (James 1:13–15)

But don't despair, dear sisters, God knows our fragile frame. Always and forever, our God waits for us once again, bringing us into love and obedience. Having given our life to him, our salvation is secure. Our job is to listen and obey, so we may grow in grace and peace. Jesus assures us:

> My sheep listen to my voice; I know them, and they follow me. I give them eternal life, and they shall never perish; no one can snatch them out of my hand. My Father, who has given them to me, is greater than all; no one can snatch them out of my Father's hand. I and the Father are one.
>
> (John 10:27–30)

Paul assure us that God works in us and never gives up on us:

> Being confident of this, that he who began a good work in you will carry it on to completion until the day of Christ Jesus.
>
> (Philippians 1:6)

However, God gives us free will. We must obey if we wish to reap his blessings.

> Remain in me, and I will remain in you. No branch can bear fruit by itself; it must remain in the vine. Neither can you bear fruit unless you remain in me. This is to my Father's glory, that you bear much fruit, showing yourselves to be my disciples.
>
> (John 15:4, 8)

Not to say, we can never fail; guaranteed we will fail. Thus, we will experience consequences of our disobedient actions because God as a father disciplines us. We will also experience His loving forgiveness and restoration because He loves us.

Therefore, as a child clings to the hand of his father, so we must cling to the hand of our Heavenly Father through good times and bad. A child is saved from much harm and receives good by obedience to parents. We, also, receive multiple blessings by our obedience to God. He gave His word as an instruction manual for an abundant life. Not pain free, but safe and secure in His arms. Good parents are a great advantage. In this broken world, not everyone was given this gift. Even so, we have a loving God who has the attributes of both a mother and a father. He will nurture and raise us to be mature and complete lacking in nothing. Obedience to Him brings blessings, disobedience to Him brings consequences.

> Listen to the quiet, friends. Oh look, a scampering squirrel jumping from one tree to another. Ah! The soothing sound of a bubbling brook. A moment of pure joy, forgetting our sorrows. ~ **Prayer:** Lord, draw us close to you so we will desire to obey you. Cultivate an ability in us to see the glass as half full instead of half empty. Teach us to sing praises despite the hard times.

Hide in My Heart: "We love because he first loved us," (1 John 4:19). "The man who looks intently I into the perfect law that gives freedom and continues to do this, not forgetting what he has heard, but doing it, he will be blessed in what he does," (James 1:25).
Choose Today: I understand, obedience to God brings blessings, disobedience brings consequences. As for me, I choose God's way.

Week 20, Day 2. Read: Chapter John 14.
Journal: Underline the verses that call out to you, then journal his teachings.
Action Tool: "We love because he first loved us," (1 John 4:19). Concentrate this week on loving others first. Write the verse on an index card and post it on your refrigerator.

Week 20, Day 3. Read: Chapter John 15.
Journal: Underline the verses that call out to you, then journal his teachings.
Action Tool: List on index card 10 ways you have experienced love. Post it on your car vizor and review it each time you start up the car.

Week 20, Day 4. Read: 1 John 4:7–21.
Journal: Consider how well you were loved as a child and the means of discipline your parents used. Now contrast that with God's way of love and discipline.
Action Tool: On index card list 10 ways you show love. Are you loving first (not expecting anything back, just reaching out in love, no matter the others response)?

Week 20, Day 5. Read: James 1:22–25.
Journal: In what ways do you resist obedience? Is your obedience out of fear, duty or love? Pray for a deep yearning to obey God.
Action Tool: Letters of Love. Hand-write a letter of love. Caution, do not use this note for correction or instruction but as an instrument of praise, expressing that which you enjoy, appreciate and love about this person. Mail it to them (not email).

Heart of a Pilgrim
Week 21, Day 1

For God so loved the world that he gave his one and only Son, so that whoever believes in him shall not perish but have eternal life.

(John 3:16)

> Monica, my daughter, you have journeyed up the Mountain of Gloom a good number of times. Will you share with the pilgrims, as we idle a while here on the Hills of Hope, your story of being loved before you learned to love? It may be a comfort to some of our sisters.

"My story is complicated. My life is complicated, and I am complicated. I want to be like my grandmother. My grandmother, Virginia Watson Schneider, was an amazing woman of God. My mother and grandmother traveled to Romania, found me and rescued me from the Casa de Copi, where hundreds of us toddlers were warehoused. She chose me when I was three years old living in the Romanian orphanage. She loved me before she even knew me.

As I am writing this, I am listening to "I Choose You" by Sara Barellieas.

> My whole heart will be yours forever
> This is a beautiful start
> To a lifelong love letter
> Tell the world that we finally got it all right
> I choose you
> I will become yours and you will become mine
> I choose you

This song reminds me so much of my grandmother and her love for me. My grandmother had a huge heart. She loved me from the moment she laid eyes on me. I always her unconditional love. Even when I was bad, she didn't criticize me with harsh words, but instead spoke words of wisdom and encouragement. She never made me feel like I wasn't wanted.

Being adopted, I often felt like I was a nobody, a reject. I felt like I was always being passed off to someone because I was too complicated. Grandma never passed me off. She stuck with me to make sure I succeeded. She helped me realize I was valuable. To this day, when things get rough for me, I try to listen to my grandmother's voice saying, "You are loved; you are perfect." Grandma was someone who understood me for who I am, not what I should be. I learned to trust because she was always there for me. She taught me how to love because she loved me.

We had fun times. I remember after home school, she would take me to ice-skating lessons, then Taco Bell for lunch. She treated me like a princess. Grandma died when I was thirteen.

I want to be like my Grandma. She had a huge heart and a love for others. I want to help others see the love God has for us. My goal is to be a light in this world for a child in need. She is my hero. I want to be just like her."

> Thank you, sweetie. Grandma was indeed a loving woman and you are growing to be like her. We were blessed to have her in our lives giving us an example of selfless love. Not everyone is so fortunate. Modeling ourselves after a Godly woman is a great idea! The Bible is full of roll-models, especially Jesus who gave his life for us. Tomorrow, ladies, we will pass by Council Rock. Can't wait to hear what the Lord will teach us there.

Prayer: Abba, you have taught us to love by loving us. Some folks did not have loving families, therefore, are not good at loving others. We thank you for the love that has come our way. Teach us to be loving and selfless. Amen.

Hide in My Heart: "My command is this: Love each other as I have loved you. Greater love has no one than this that he lay down his life for his friends" (John 15:12–13).
Choose Today: I choose, by the strength of my Jesus, to become love in action.

Week 21, Day 2. Read: 1 Corinthians 13:1–7.
Journal: What are your love wounds and how do they interfere with your giving love?
Action Tool: Learn the language of love for your family members.

- ❖ Think over how a family member feels loved? Is it through little gifts, through words of affection or encouragement, by being serving, through food, etc.?
- ❖ If you do not know, ask him/her, or observe and figure it out.
- ❖ Speak love to this person today by an act of love in the way they best receive it.

Week 21, Day 3. Reread: 1 Corinthians 13:1–7.
Journal: Circle the words that are your strengths for love in action. How do you show these strengths?
Action Tool: Plan a specific action using a love-strength this week.

Week 21, Day 4. Read: John 15:12–13.
Journal: How is love in action "laying down your life"? What love in action is difficult for you?
Action Tool: Choose a person for whom you carry a record of wrongs. Figuratively, scrunch the list and cast it into the sea. Or write the list on a paper and burn it. Affirm aloud, "Today, will have its own troubles so, by God's power, I refuse to carry the past record of wrongs with me into the future."

Week 21, Day 5. Read: 1 Corinthians 13: 8–13.
Journal: How is God asking you to express faith, hope and love amid your circumstance? How does doing so bring you joy in the midst?
Action Tool: Go to the library and check out, <u>The Five Love Languages: How to Express Heartfelt Commitment to Your Mate</u>, by Gary Chapman.

Council Rock
Week 22, Day 1

First, seek the counsel of the Lord.

(1 Kings 22:5)

> This way, dear ones, to Council Rock. The elders of the native Indians would sit upon this rock to share their wisdom with young braves. Wrinkles were a sign of wisdom. Now, that sounds good. I must be wise by now since I have an abundance of wrinkles. Shall we enjoy a lunch break while we ponder the council of the aged?

The Lord our God, Creator of the Universe, Savior and Father spoke wisdom through the Bible. It is amazing how the words for life, not death, for joy amid struggles, are all contained within.

> All scripture is God breathed and is useful for teaching, rebuking, correcting and training in righteousness so that the man of God may be thoroughly equipped for every good work.
>
> (2 Timothy 3:16–17)

Therefore, it is important to concentrate on allowing God's word to penetrate your heart and mind. Do not go it alone or rest on your own wisdom or opinion. Do not take my opinion (or anyone else's) as truth. Sift all decisions through the truth of scripture.

> Do not quench the Spirit. Do not treat prophecies with contempt but test them all; hold on to what is good, reject every kind of evil.
>
> (1 Thessalonians 5:19–22)

Rely on the counsel of the Holy Spirit.

> I will ask the Father and he will give you another Counselor to be with you forever the Spirit of truth. The world cannot accept Him because it neither sees him nor knows Him. But you know Him, for He lives with you and will be in you.
> (John 14:16–17)

> If any of you lack wisdom, he should ask God, who gives generously to all without finding fault and it will be given to him.
> (James 1:5)

Then seek the counsel of men and women who have shown maturity in Christ.

> Plans fail for lack of counsel, but with many advisors, they succeed.
> (Psalms 15:22)

Review the decision with scriptural wisdom.

> But the wisdom that comes from heaven is first of all pure; then peace-loving, considerate, submissive, full of mercy and good fruit, impartial and sincere.
> (James 3:17)

If married, pray that God will give you one mind with your husband. Wait for peace and Godly wisdom before moving forward.

> Therefore, if you have any encouragement from being united with Christ, if any comfort from his love, if any common sharing in the Spirit, if any tenderness and compassion, then make my joy complete by being like-minded, having the same love, being *one in spirit and of one mind.*
> (Philippians 2:1-2)

Believe me, once my husband and I learned to stop badgering each other into agreement, our marriage had less strife. We learned to seek Godly counsel from scripture, in prayer and through mature Christians before a decision. God is of one mind, not divided. Therefore, a Christian husband and wife both waiting upon the Holy Spirit will come to one mind.

> The way of a fool seems right to him, but a wise man (woman) listens to advice.
> (Proverbs 12:15)

At first, issues with my husband were impossible to discuss without anger. We each thought the other needed to change. God showed us how our selfish natures hindered oneness. Through counsel, we applied scripture to our own thinking, instead of concentrating on convincing our spouse. I realized that whenever I tried to argue with my prone-to-argue husband, he became increasingly concrete in his resistance. My stubbornness also cemented.

God enabled me to release "my right" to have the last say. I offer my opinion, then submit to God to bring my husband to the best decision. Not necessarily my way, but God's way. Sometimes, husbands make poor decisions that affect us or our children. Even then we must trust God to work it together for good. Thus, we enable our husband to function as the God ordained head of the family.

> Wives submit to your husbands as to the Lord. For the husband is the head of the wife as Christ is the head of the church.
> (Ephesians 5:22–23)

Over time, when I prayed for God's wisdom and oneness of mind, we began to agree. He began to change. I changed. Sometimes, my husband's opinion revised, sometimes mine, but either way there was now peace between us. We learned to wait for agreement, no one dominating the other.

> Submit to one another out of reverence for Christ.
> (Ephesians 5:21)

At first, we only sought Godly counsel on major issues but now we seek God, consult scripture and one another on most decisions. However, even all these years later, I can slip into a mind-set determined to make my husband see it "my way". It still doesn't work. Prayer, yielding, waiting on the Lord does!

In this we found true harmony. It is not my husband's heavy-handed rule, which I resent, nor my stubborn determination to secure my rights, which he resents. We seek oneness of mind and direction brought about by the Holy Spirit in which we both find rest. Added benefit… if we misjudge, have false wisdom (which can happen because we are imperfect) or if the results are painful and difficult to bear, we cannot blame one another, for the decision was made in oneness with Godly counsel. Praise God.

These Biblical precepts are the mesh to use for sifting all decisions through the truth of scripture. No peace and good fruit, no agreement in the spirit, then no action. Wait?

> Are any of you stubborn like me? Or am I the only one? It is often hard to hear wisdom because of the rebuttal in our brain. I learned to listen beneath my husband's intense tone of voice to the wisdom of his words. Letting go of my pride, I accepted the possibility that I might be wrong. My husband, over the years, learned to trust my insights. Only then, could we hear the council of the wise, of scripture, or the still small voice of God.

Prayer: Lord, it is amazing that we can receive counsel through the maker of the universe. Thank you, Almighty God, for sharing your wisdom. Attune our hearts and minds to listen and obey your counsel. In Jesus name, Amen.

Hide in My Heart: "The wisdom that comes from heaven is first of all pure; then peace-loving, considerate, submissive, full of mercy and good fruit, impartial and sincere" (James 3:17).

Choose Today: I choose to listen to the Holy Spirit teaching, convicting and revealing wisdom.

Week 22, Day 2. Read: John 14:15–18 and 1 Thessalonians 5:19–22.
Journal: In what ways do you quench the spirit?
Action Tool: Quenching means to pour water on a fire, putting it out. We put out the flame of the Holy Spirit through disobedience and hard heartedness. We do not lose our salvation but lose our ability to forgive, be strong, obedient and receive His joy, peace and self-control.

1. When you require a decision lift your right index finger as a *Signal* to ask God for wisdom. Practice on small decisions so you remember on big decisions.
2. Lift your finger again as a *Signal* to wait upon "oneness of mind." Express your opinion without demands, and then wait upon the Lord to bring unity through the Holy Spirit.
3. RAISED INDEX FINGER; Pray for wisdom. Wait for oneness of mind.

Week 22, Day 3. Read: Ephesians 5:21–33.
Journal: When you and your husband decide together, do you badger, argue, manipulate, get passive aggressive to get your own way? What technique does your husband or a loved one use? How might you seek "oneness of mind", "submitting one to another", and to the wisdom of God?
Action Tool: Use this week's memory verse, James 3:17 to sift a sample decision.

Week 22, Day 4. Read: 1 Kings 22:5, James 1:5, Proverbs 12:15 and 19:20.
Journal: Is your "being right" more important than wisdom? How do you first seek the counsel of God?
Action Tool: Make a list of wise counselors God has provided for you. Include pastors, friends, business professionals, and any other people God places on your heart. Include your spouse!

Week 22, Day 5. Read: 1 Corinthians 12:4–11.
Journal: Is God divided on his instructions? Why is seeking "oneness of mind" between a husband and wife on decisions so important? What is the first step necessary for you and your husband to move in this direction?
Action Tool: Steps to Seek God's Oneness of Mind

- ❖ Offer opinion
- ❖ Pray about it together
- ❖ Let it rest
- ❖ Pray separately
- ❖ Apply God's word
- ❖ Wait for oneness of mind as led by God

Log Cabin Home
Week 23, Day 1

> **She is clothed in with strength and dignity; she can laugh at the days to come. She speaks with wisdom, and faithful instruction is on her tongue.**
> **(Proverbs 31:25–26)**

> Oh look, girls, at the rustic little log house over there! Must have been a miner's shack. Come, let's peek inside. Hey, someone carved names on the wall, "Henry and Edith Strong". Wonder if Edith liked living so remote? Sometimes, an isolated woodland cottage is appealing.

Stroll a wooded lane, through little gate in a picket fence; stop to pick a flower in the dainty garden. Open the cottage door into a warm, sunny living room filled with happy family and friends. Ah, the smell of roasted chicken and just baked bread awaken the taste buds. Laughter tickles your ears; the love of the Lord fills your heart. This is home… or rather the home I wish myself to be.

Imagining my inner self as a house and garden, this comfortable scene represents my fantasy. If you open the door and peek inside me, I want you to discover beauty, warmth, sunshine, and enticing fragrances. I yearn for the love of Jesus to flow forth from me to you, lifting your day when you are in my presence. That is my heart's desire.

Here is the reality. Stumble up a weed filled gravel driveway, stop to pick a rose from a tangled bush, open the door into a sunny living room, cluttered with papers, shoes, dogs and dishes in the sink. Ah, the fragrance of roasted chicken and home baked bread tickles your senses while angry words assault your ears! This is the real inside me. It is lovely and thorny, warm and messy, loving and angry, typical and unique.

> The wise woman builds her house, but with her own hands, the foolish one tears hers down.
>
> (Proverbs 14: 1)

How does your house look? Let us confront ourselves with the disparity between who we want to be versus the reality of our inner self.

Test time... Circle the answer that best illustrates you.

1. <u>Do you judge yourself by the word of God rather than comparing yourself to others?</u>
   a. I always do as the Bible directs and am never influenced by what other people think.
   b. I strive to do as God leads even when others do not understand, approve or appreciate my actions.
   c. I want to be conformed to Christlikeness, but it is way beyond my ability, so I just cling to the hope of God's word.
   d. I am so much better than the general populace; I am fine the way I am.

2. <u>Do you put his word into action in your daily life?</u>
   a. I am focused on God all day, every day without exception. Christian duty requires a morning quiet time, and so I seldom miss mine.
   b. My habit pattern is to greet the day with prayer, memorize scripture, and try to remember during the day to rely on God's word.
   c. Morning is great for starting out focused on God, but I am too busy to think of Him during the day. More-often-than-not, I do as I've always done.
   d. You can't expect me to count it all joy when I suffer and to bless those who curse me. Hey, I'm not Jesus!

3. <u>Do you love others with patience, kindness, trust, truth, self-sacrifice, and perseverance?</u>
   a. Yes, of course. I do not understand why it is hard for other people.

b. I confront myself with these qualities, asking God to change and grow me, and be a conduit of His love.
   c. I hope to love with selflessness, but my selfishness always jumps in resulting in unloving behavior.
   d. Patience (kindness, etc.) is so difficult to sustain that I stopped praying about it. If I pray for patience, life just gets tougher. It is too hard, so I give up.

4. <u>Do you recognize your own self-centeredness and deny yourself to serve God?</u>
   a. I am not self-centered in the least. In fact, I am the one everyone counts on to serve.
   a. I seek to serve others, willingly laying down my rights in accordance with God's word.
   a. I have the desire to do what is good, but I cannot carry it out consistently.
   a. My self-esteem is low, so I must build it up by focusing on what is important to me. Besides, I am not a doormat for others to walk over.

Which letter did you circle most? If you circled "a", consider in prayer whether your answers reflect holding yourself in too high a regard. Perhaps, you view others with intolerance for not living up to God's standards. Perhaps some answers were "a" because 1) It is easy to be a "nice person" due to your personality; 2) You are protecting yourself with bravado, good works, or legalism to feel better about yourself; 3) You are blind to your faults. God says,

> For all have sinned and fall short of the glory of God and are justified freely by his grace through the redemption that came by Jesus Christ.
> (Romans 3: 23-24).

I can relate to these "a" answer folks as there was a time when I believed no anger existed in me. I was a moral, loving person with little fault. And I was! But I was, also, blind to my selfish, prideful, passive-aggressive nature.

It took my husband, children and much prayer to reveal the truth about my inner being and for me to yield to Godly change.

I can, also, relate to those who answered "d" for these are the pity pit folks! The step from "I am so good," to "It's not my fault. Woe is me," happens easily and quickly.

If your answers were mostly "b" or "c", congratulations, you are being conformed to the image of Christ. Atta Girl! The ability to shine forth as loving, gracious women, empty of resentments and ready to serve comes through faith in Jesus Christ. We must not be blind to our sinful nature, nor just give up and wallow, but realize we are strugglers depending on Christ to work his miracle of change within us.

Don't despair if you have a long way to travel to be a loving Godly woman. It takes a lifetime. The whole purpose of this test is to see ourselves clearly, to see our need for Jesus. Only then can we humbly submit to dependence on Him to work in us. God will not give up on you. He is molding you into a woman of God. All you must be is willing!

> And we know that in all things God works for the good of those who love him, who have been called according to his purpose. For those God foreknew he also predestined to be conformed to the likeness of his Son, that he might be the firstborn among many brothers.
>
> (Romans 8:28–29)

Let's sit awhile in Edith's front yard and think about the home in our heart. Who wants to invite us for dinner at your house? No fair tidying up first. This is a Come-as-you-are Party.

Prayer: Abba, create in me a home you are proud to live in, a place of comfort and peace. Work in me to develop a gentle and quiet spirit. In Jesus name. Amen

Hide in My Heart: "Your beauty should not come from outward adornment, such as braided hair and the wearing of gold jewelry and fine clothes. Instead, it should be that of your inner self, the unfading beauty of a *gentle and quiet spirit* which is of great worth in God's sight," (1 Peter 3:3–4).

Choose Today: I choose to allow God to create a lovely, welcoming home within me.

Week 23, Day 2. Read: Proverbs 31:10–31.
Journal and Action Tool: Home in my Heart
Sit still with your eyes closed. Visualize the ideal home that is you. Walk into the front yard, into the house. What do you smell and see? How does it feel? How is your countenance? Describe your *ideal* picture of your inner self as a house/home. Be specific, illustrating the house details plus the feelings and mood of the home.
Remember, the picture is the God-transformed YOU. This God-transformed you may be far from whom you are today. Stay focused on a picture of you as a woman God created you to be. Imagine love flowing through you, God's love to those who enter your home. You are a woman clothed with strength and dignity, wisdom and faithful instruction, a gentle and quiet spirit. You are of great worth to God.

Week 23, Day 3. Read: Romans 3:23–24 and Romans 8:28–29.
Journal: We will never be perfect. We are a work in progress with God as our carpenter. Review the a) and b) answers from the lesson today and journal your response.
Action Tool: Print out a picture that represents your "ideal house". Make single word notes on the picture that remind you of the "new inner you". Tuck it in your bible or post it on your wall. Hold this image in your heart and revisit it until it becomes the real you.

Week 23, Day 4. Read: Proverbs 14:1.
Journal: What can you celebrate today in your "home" both spiritual and physical?
Action Tool: Plan a moment of celebration. For example, raise a glass of orange juice for a toast of thanksgiving for… (whatever quality you are celebrating).

Week 23, Day 5. Read: Romans 12:9–13, I Peter 4:7–11.
Journal: When you allow others to see your house Just-As-It-Is, you give them a gift. They are now free to share their house Just-As-It-Is. That is real hospitality; welcoming folks just as you are. The warmth of the welcome, not perfection of the house means most. Are you hospitable? What prevents you from opening your physical home to others? How can you create a more welcoming home?
Joy Trail: Share a meal. Buy frozen lasagna and packaged salad, then invite friends into your home. Pain makes us withdraw; find joy by doing the opposite.

Disappointment Slew
Week 24, Day 1

Then you will know that I am the Lord; those who hope in me will not be disappointed.

(Isaiah 49:23b)

Oh, my feet hurt. A soak in the cold river will be sensational. The miners named this part of the river "Disappointment Slew" because it did not yield gold. Perhaps, that is why Edith and Henry left their cabin home. Disappointment can sure erode our faith and joy in life.

"God better do something great, or I'm done with him!" spew my son, anguished, frustrated and angry at God. Here is an excerpt from my journal entry, years ago when my son expressed his angst. "After years of praying and being faithful, my son still sees no results for a career, a Godly wife, a sense of purpose. From my perspective now as an aged woman, I expect God will do something great. However, it may not be what my son expects. He may need to experience walking without his God. Still I am confident, God will do something great in my son's life because this man is his own."

Anguish over never-ending struggles is familiar. Frustrated with God, we strike out on our own. Consequences result with long-lasting repercussions. Consider the Israelites and Arab conflicts. God promised Abraham a son. After many years, tired of waiting, Sarah offered Abraham her servant to bear a child. Thus, Abraham bore a child with Hagar who became the father of Arab nations. The promised son through Sarah, born later, became the father of the Israelites. God's timing differed from Sarah's timing. The results of not waiting on God have reverberated throughout the centuries in the continuing hostility between Abraham's two lines of ancestors, the Arabs and Israeli.

When disappointed, we perceive, as Sarah, that God didn't keep His promise. We do not understand the wait. God appears to be inactive and indifferent. How can I go on trusting? How can I find peace amid this? O my God, you are silent and distant. Do you not care? Do you hear my prayers?

> How long, O Lord? Will you forget me forever? How long will you hide your face from me? How long must I wrestle with my thoughts and every day have sorrow in my heart?
> (Psalm 13 1-2)

It is hard to hang on to hope when disappointments prevail. Yet hanging on is exactly what Christ enables us to do. Persevere, cling to hope. Choose to trust, even when it does not make sense. Grab ahold of hope when we find no reason to hope. He calls out, "Cling to my life ring!" Our hands are numb from holding on. Still, we cling.

> Why do you complain my way is hidden from the Lord; my cause is disregarded by my God?' Do you not know? Have you not heard? The Lord is the everlasting God, the Creator of the ends of the earth. He will not grow tired or weary and his understanding no one can fathom. He gives strength to the weary and increases the power of the weak. Even youths grow tired and weary and young men stumble and fall; but those who hope in the Lord will renew their strength. They will soar on wings like eagles; they will run and not grow weary; they will walk and not be faint.
> (Isaiah 40: 27–31)

Having no control over the circumstances, seeing no hope for change, and God being so long to respond, causes us to despair. Faltering, we cry out and He, once again, throws us the life ring of hope.

> But I will trust in your unfailing love.
> (Psalm 13:5)

I remain confident of this: I will see the goodness of the Lord in the land of the living. Wait for the Lord; be strong and take heart and wait for the Lord.

(Psalm 27:13–14)

Ah, soaking my feet was refreshing, as is the water of life and hope in Jesus. Just to update you, ladies, now several years later, my son has a career job he enjoys, a wife whom he loves, a renewed walk with God, and much joy in his heart. Isn't our God good? Let's make it a short day and build a campfire.

Prayer: Lord, we live here, in a finite world so waiting feels forever. Keep us focused on you, Father, while we wait. Don't let us give up. We claim your strength to endure. Amen.

Hide in My Heart: "Trust in the Lord with all your heart and lean not on your own understanding. In all your ways acknowledge Him and He will make your paths straight," (Proverbs 3:5–6).

Choose Today: "I remain confident of this: I will see the goodness of the Lord in the land of the living," (Psalm 27:13).

Week 24, Day. Read: Psalm 13:1–2.
Journal: Pour out your disappointment in God. What has quenched your hope? How have the promises in scripture failed to line up with your reality? In what circumstances have seen no response from Him?
Action Tool: Be prepared to wait. While you are waiting get busy clinging by memorizing scripture and serving others.

Week 24, Day 3. Read: Isaiah 40:27–31 and Matthew 16:15–17.
Journal: Who do you say He is?
Action Tool: Buy a bead bracelet from a Christian bookstore (or make one yourself from a bead shop) that has the word, "Pray" on it. Pray through the day. Ask God to do something great in your life.

Week 24, Day 4. Read: Psalm 13:5, Psalm 27:13–14 and Proverbs 3:5.
Journal: Affirm that, though you do not understand, and despite what you feel, you will cling to and hope in the Lord. You will eagerly await his path for you.
Action Tool: Look and rejoice in the *greatness* of your life today, without any changes. List 10 items.

Week 24, Day 5. Read: Proverbs 21:21 and 1 Thessalonians 1:2–10.
Journal: How might you pursue righteousness and "life" today while you are "waiting"?
Joy Trail: Count your blessings. When someone asks you, "How are you?" respond, "Thankful."

Camp Fire Chat
Week 25, Day 1

So, do not fear, for I am with you; do not be dismayed, for I am your God. I will strengthen you and help you; I will uphold you with my righteous right hand.
(Isaiah 41:10)

> Popcorn anyone? Settle down around the campfire and take turns shaking the Jiffy Pop. Today while we trekked along, Kathi asked to learn more of my story. For your encouragement, with my husband's approval, here's the tale of my prince turned ogre turned hero. So here goes.

On the third day of our honeymoon, my new husband revealed his temper. Not all at once but bit by bit, starting with irritation over some small matter (Maui onions versus regular onions), which escalated into angry argumentative words. It devastated me! Why would my God, whom I trusted, do this to me? During our year of courtship, Gene treated me like a princess. He fastened my ski boots, helped paint my house, brought me little presents and baked pies for me. Different from the other Christian guys I dated, he bathed me with the word of God. He maintained sexual purity. At thirty-three, now devoted to my Lord, I determined Gene as God's man for me. You understand my dismay when my prince turned ogre.

For my husband's New York Italian family, explosive arguments and put-downs were normal; their way of life. I come from a California German-English family who stowed anger. I took every put-down from Gene to heart, trying my best to do and be everything he wanted. Never enough. Always something else, some new reason to be angry. No physical abuse, but many devastating words. I couldn't believe the unkind words he and his mom exchanged on the phone. For me each hurtful word threw a grenade to my confidence and to my faith in God.

I seethed with anger at the God I had trusted to bring me a loving husband. My lowest point came one dreary day. Curled up in a closet, I gnawed on my hand and wished I could die. Married three months, I knew a divorce was the only answer. What had happened to my prince? What happened to my faith? Exhibiting passive aggressive anger in many spiteful ways, I also began yelling. We had moments of peace, but more often pain.

In our kitchen, a while later, I leaned against the sink, screaming at Gene about who knows what. On this day, Gene remained calm and centered on the Lord, which I must tell you I hated. I hated his being right with the Lord one day and explosive the next. It left me off balance. My prince stood in the kitchen that day when I talked about divorce. His eyes expressed love. He told me, "I do not want to be like my family. I want to be God's man. We will get help. Whatever is needed." Gene continued to be repentant and work on change through-out the years. Whatever the setbacks, whatever his explosion, when he calmed down, he was repentant and determined to mature in exemplifying the fruits of the spirit. Without his willingness and efforts, I would not have stayed.

Yet, he wasn't the only one who needed to change. In counseling and Bible study, I learned to cope with my passive aggressive anger, disappointment, depression and negative self-talk. A loving response, no matter Gene's behavior became my goal. I learned not to accept abusive words directed at me. Those were his issues not mine. I needed to separate out my issues and work on those.

Forgiveness had to stay fresh and frequent. Gene and I retreated alone together twice a year. We planned special surprise moments. We talked over everything even when it hurt. We became Christian retreat junkies to get away from our spouse and have a weekend of peace. Separating for an hour or a few days, we put ourselves on time out when needed. Cultivating forgiveness enabled us to come back together seeking to love. Not easy, nor quick. Often, it felt as if I did all the changing. Add in the dynamics of seven miscarriages, one live birth (our son), then later our adopted wounded daughter, and, oh my, it was hard. But life is hard. As long as we stayed together willing to try, seeking unity despite the turmoil, then I believed it would be worth the effort. Even when I could not see it.

Fast forward many years and many tears. My husband and I have become one. He is my best friend. I share everything with him. Our love grew deep. We are like two comfortable old shoes. Our temperaments and outlook on life are still very different. He is still prone to loud intense conversations yet has learned not to attack or blame me for his reactions or circumstances. I have learned to speak up and not stow my feeling, taking care of my own mental health with restorative time when necessary. We seek to deal with stress in constructive ways, getting into nature as often as possible, and spending time with God.

Even so yesterday, Gene said, "Blue!" in an intense, nasty, corrective tone of voice when I described our car on the phone. That one word hooked me. When I got off the phone, I lit into him like a dog tearing apart a stuffed squeaky toy. I wanted an apology, and he didn't want to give one. We exploded over one silly word! God finally got my attention and put me in my room on time out. I prayed and let go, ready to come out of my room as God's woman. I apologized for my overreaction; Gene did as well. We hugged and went about our day in peace.

Please understand, dear friends, this is my journey and yours may be different. My husband and I were ready to change though it took many years. We both worked on our own issues and forgiveness. Did following Biblical instruction make a difference in my life? Well, ladies, I can say wholeheartedly, yes. Being faithful to God, following His way, has brought life out of death for me.

> Yum, I love popcorn. Worth carrying along in my pack even if some of it got a wee bit burnt. Each of you, friends, has a story God is writing in your life. Tomorrow night, I would love to hear one of yours. Ok, time to hit the sack. Last one to bed, be sure to put the campfire dead out.

Prayer: Praise your name, Father God, for being in the business of bringing life out of death. Thank you for doing this work in us even when we can't yet see it happening. Forgive our hard hearts and give us an overwhelming desire for life. Amen.

Hide in My Heart: "So do not fear, for I am with you; do not be dismayed, for I am your God. I will strengthen you and help you; I will uphold you with my righteous right hand," (Isaiah 41:10).

Choose Today: I choose to allow God to restore life out of death in me even though it is painful.

Week 25, Day 2. Read: Read: John 11:17–44.
Journal: What is dead that needs resurrection in your life?
Action Tool: Apply the "Three Day Rule".
Jesus died and was buried in the tomb for three days then rose from the dead. When something stinks with death, when you find yourself in the tomb, when your attitude is rotten, when scripture doesn't seem to penetrate, apply the "Three Day Rule".

- Tell yourself, "In three days...." "In three days, my attitude will turn around through the power of God." "In three days, circumstances will be better."
- The second night say to yourself, "Tomorrow morning, by the grace of God, I will awake with a new attitude."
- On the third day, when you awake, affirm that today you will seek life.
- As you grow stronger in your walk with God, give yourself only two days, then one day.

Week 25, Day 3. Read: Genesis 3:1–24.
Journal: How did Adam and Eve choose death over life? What were the results? Why did Eve listen to the serpent? Notice the man's response when God asked him about what happened. Did Adam take responsibility for his actions? Who did the man accuse? (Refer back to "Pillars of Shame").
Action Tool: Apply the "Three Day Rule" to something that "stinketh" in your life.

Week 25, Day 4. Read: Deuteronomy 30:11–20. Choose Life.
Journal: What do you choose? How will you choose life today?

Action Tool: Write and post, "Today I choose Life!" Read it when tempted to choose a little death.

Week 25, Day 5. Read: Isaiah 41:10.
Journal: We need strength go through the day. Fortunately, God has got our back. What do you fear? Journal your prayer against fear and for strength to meet this day.
Action Tool: Hold up your hand, symbolically reach for the hand of God and clasp it tight. You are His child; He is your Abba (daddy); trust Him to get you through.

Grumbling Gulch
Week 26, Day 1

> **Do everything without complaining or arguing, so that you may become blameless and pure, children of God, without fault in a crooked and depraved generation, in which you shine like stars in the universe**
> **(Philippians 2:14).**

> Oh, my goodness, this pack is so heavy. I'm getting too old for this. Why doesn't God get a younger woman to lead this trip? Why do I have to do it over and over again? My bones ache. And then the women think I have all the answers and I don't. They're such whiners sometimes. They haven't been through half of what I've been through and, yet they don't get this joy stuff. God, can't I go back to the Hills of Hope and you send a helicopter to lift me out. What do you say? I'm just not up for this today... Ohhhhh, my back aches, my feet hurt, and that woman over there is just irritating me to death.

There is a saying, "You are what you think about all day." Dale Carnegie, the great sales trainer, taught:

> Sow a thought, reap a habit
> Sow a habit, reap a characteristic
> Sow a characteristic, reap a destiny.

Some philosophers say, "Affirm what you want to happen, and it will happen." Others spout, "If you think you can or think you can't, you're right."

Psychologists and scientists tell us our subconscious has an imprint, neurological connections, declaring who we are and how we perceive life.

Parents help create this imprint through many years of words. Self-talk solidifies this view. Reinforcing ingrained opinions results in habitual actions. Positive connections work well for us; negative imprints subvert our good intentions and may cripple us. To change our results, we must change our subconscious patterns of thinking.

> Do not conform to the pattern of this world but be transformed by the renewing of your mind. Then you will be able to test and approve what God's will is—his good, pleasing and perfect will
>
> (Romans 12:2).

Our Jesus is the great psychologist because, being one with the creator God, he understands how we function. His word encourages us to dwell on whatever is good and excellent. God knows dwelling on the good will empower us.

> Finally, brothers and sisters, whatever is true, whatever is noble, whatever is right, whatever is pure, whatever is lovely, whatever is admirable—if anything is excellent or praiseworthy—think about (dwell on) such things.
>
> (Philippians 4:8)

A propensity to dwell on the negative saps' motivation, energy and joy. There is always, always, always a reason and excuse for depression or negativity. After all, life is hard. Yet, which one of these depressing issues will change for the better by endlessly cycling around in your head? We waste our mental energy trying to control such things. For example: advanced illness or bad decisions of a loved one, accidents, or hostility around the world. Some issues exist out of our control. If you can't solve a problem, let it go. Our pastor illustrated, "We think by worrying we are doing something constructive. We are showing we care. The truth is worry, without action toward a resolution debilitates."

So, grumbling, self-put-downs, and endless worry or anxiety are good only as a call to motivate us to action. A general negative countenance is not only fruitless, it is destructive. It also continues to cement into our subconscious brain that life is just awful, we are rotten, depressed, stupid (pick one or add your own) and today will not be a good day or the next day either. And so, our character continues to develop along set patterns of selfish ungodliness. Our God, dedicated to molding our character, must give us one more lesson, one more opportunity to choose righteous thinking and hope. A mental habit of focusing on the bad creates a miserable destiny.

A wonderful song, "Walkin' Sinai," written by Al Poirier ©1974 Lillenas Publishing Co., sung by Dan Whittmore, says it all:

> Well, don't you know that in the days of old,
> When the Israelites didn't do what they were told…
> Our Lord, simply told them this,
> Go on and take another lap around Mount Sinai,
> Till you learn your lesson,
> Till you stop you're whinin' and you quit your rebellin'
> Till you learn to stand in your day of testin'
> By trustin' and obeyin' the Lord.

Take a moment and listen to Dan singing the song by going to this link and scrolling down to "Walkin' Sinai": http://www.danwhittemore.com/my_songs

God's word says:

> Do everything without complaining or arguing, so that you may become blameless and pure, children of God, without fault in a crooked and depraved generation, in which you shine like stars in the universe.
> (Philippians 2:14)

If our self-talk is negative, if our observations about life are always a downer, if you concentrate on what we think God has not done, you will never arise from misery. Therefore, since God knows what is best for us, and He asks us not to be complaining whiners, we need to change our stinkin' thinkin'. As you think, so you will be. Where do you want your thoughts to live? It is your choice. God has given you self-control as a gift of his Holy Spirit. He has given you his word and promises. He has, also, given you freewill to choose each moment where to dwell, in futility and depression or in joy and peace.

"Yeah, right!" you say sarcastically. "Easier said than done! My mind just takes its own trips without any help from me. It would take a more powerful person than me to change my way of thinking. Hearing the truth just isn't enough, I need help!"

Yes, you need help. God has supplied that help through the Holy Spirit in your own being. This week, we will explore just how powerful God has created words to be. Changing the imprint of our subconscious to be positive and hopeful despite the circumstances, by trusting in God, not man, begins today... if you are willing.

> Yes, Lord, I hear you. This climb, again and again, is for my benefit, not just for the ladies coming along. I need another lap around the mountain until I stop my grumbling and put on praise. Yes, Lord, I can do it. Yes, I will count your strength, moment by moment, to get me up and over. Ok, you and me, Lord. I'm standing up now, ugha. I'm putting the pack on, ooha. Trusting and obeying the Lord.

Prayer: Lord, you spoke the world into being and blew life into man. You gave us, also, the power to speak life or death. We give our words so little meaning, Father, yet you say our words are like a small rudder that turns a mighty ship. Give us insight, Lord, into our own words. Thank you for your guidance, O Lord. Amen.

Hide in My Heart: "I can do everything through Him who gives me strength," (Philippians 4:13).

Choose Today: With God's power, I lay down grumbling and negative self-talk and put on thanksgiving and positive self-talk.

Week 26, Day 2. Read: Philippians, Chapter 4.

Action Tool: Substantiate the power God has provided you through simple words with the following exercise. You will need a partner. The bigger and stronger your partner, the more vivid the illustration.

1. Tell him to hold one arm up straight out to his side.
2. Place both your hands flat on his arm.
3. Tell him to repeat the words, "No, no, no," out loud while you press down on his arm as hard as you can.
4. Watch his arm go down. If he is very strong and you are weak, it may go down just a little, but it *will go down*.
5. Next, ask him to put his arm back up, straight out to his side.
6. Place both your hands flat on his arm.
7. Tell him to repeat the words, "Yes, yes, yes," out loud while you press down on his arm as hard as you can.
8. Watch his arm. It will not budge or go down, no matter how hard you press. If he is weak and you are strong, it may move a little, but you will notice how much more powerful he is, when he says the simple word, "Yes."
9. Repeat this exercise with five more people until you become convinced this is not a fluke. The simple word, "No", spoken to our self, defeats us. The simple word, "Yes", spoken to our self, empowers us.

Journal: What does this exercise and today's scripture tell you about the power God has given your words?

Week 26, Day 3. Read: Philippians 2:14 and Philippians 4:8.
Journal: List the typical negative self-talk in which you indulge. Counteract these with a list of positive, God-inspired, self-talk phrases to counter the negative that comes unbidden into your mind.
Action Tool: Replace negative thoughts with these Biblical truths:

1. YES! I can do this. I can do all things through Christ who strengthens me!
2. YES! I am more than a conqueror through him who loves me. Praise God!

Week 26 Day 4 Read: Philippians 4:13.
Journal: What do you habitually grumble about? What new thoughts will enable a habit change? Be specific such as: Put-Off grumbling about my job; Put-On being thankful I have a job.
Action Tool: Apply "Yes, Yes" to some situation today.

Week 26, Day 5. Read: James 5:7–12.
Journal: How does patience and perseverance stop grumbling? How does a simple, "Yes", empower you?
Joy Trail: Cheerful self-talk. Speak encouragement to yourself. Say "Yes, with God's help I can cope. Yes, I can have joy again. Yes, I will find the goodness of God in the land of the living."

Contemplation Meadow
Week 27, Day 1

> **Do not conform any longer to the pattern of this world but be transformed by the renewing of your mind. Then you will be able to test and approve what God's will is—his good, pleasing and perfect will.**
> **(Romans 12:2)**

> Here in the meadow this morning, watch the deer nibble the grasses. See the prairie dogs pop up out of holes, and stare at you, little paws begging. What a wonderful quiet place for contemplation and renewing our minds.

Once leaving the gentle environment of your mother's womb what cruel stresses bombarded you? What subconscious dictation controls your daily reaction to life? How is this inner voice in direct opposition to the voice of God? As we contemplate here, let God speak to the ingrained thought patterns that produce your vision of life, your reaction to people and circumstances.

God does not minimize troubles and sorrows. He does not request us to deny our feelings or pretend we are fine. Nor to stuff it and trudge on. God transforms us to embrace hope, strength, trust and victory despite the circumstances.

> If anyone is in Christ, he is a new creation; the old has gone, the new has come!
> (2 Corinthians 5:17)

Previously, we looked at the power of spoken words to create and destroy. Today, we focus on the subconscious where both destructive and creative thoughts originate.

Many ancient religions include meditation as the process to peace and joy. Jesus also, took himself away to a quiet place to pray to be refreshed. Monks spent time in quiet contemplation. Nuns spent hours doing the rosary, repeating prayers to the Lord. As it turns out, the discoveries of modern science confirm a time of quiet contemplation is significant in bringing about wholeness or as the Bible puts it "restoring our soul". Sitting quietly memorizing and affirming scripture changes the ruts (neurotransmitters) of our habitual thinking. Of course, God knew it all along.

In our current day of constant sound and hurry-scurry, we have lost this art of quiet contemplation. Constant media replaces quiet moments of solitude. Frenetic activity assaults our day eliminating the time our subconscious needs to restore health and well-being. Selecting a peaceful corner, focusing on God, filling our minds with whatever is good and excellent, our body relaxes, our mind becomes peaceful, creativity flows.

> Do not conform to the pattern of this world but be transformed by the renewing of your mind. Then you will be able to test and approve what God's will is—his good, pleasing and perfect will.
>
> (Romans 12:2)

To expedite transformation of your mind from habitual negative ruts to positive new habitual thoughts:

- ❖ Step away from the turmoil of life.
- ❖ Focus on prayer and scripture.
- ❖ Affirm the truth of God for your life.

By repetitive affirmation of scripture, we retrain the neurotransmitters in our subconscious brain to a new pattern. For example:

> <u>Negative</u> self-centered inner voice: "My life is the pits. God doesn't care and won't help me."

> Prayer: Lord, change me within.
> Scripture: "I have come that they may have life and have it to the full", (John 10:10b)
> Godly affirmation: "I am living an abundant life, by the grace of God. Contentment abides in me."

We can claim these things because Jesus said he came to give us abundant life. He does not promise us a rousing financial success or a perfect love life, and yet, He promises fullness of life as His grace bestows. He promises that within His abundance, we can be content, even if our finances are meager. Seek to renew your mind by meditating (reading, pondering, reciting out loud) on His truths. Replace your corrupted inner belief with a Godly healing inner belief. Transform negative voices to scripture filled voices.

Another example:
> Negative self-centered inner voice: "I am too tired. I can't do this right now. It doesn't matter. Who cares? I give up."
> Prayer: Lord, change me to be a person of action even when it overwhelms me.
> Scripture: "I can do all things through Christ who strengthen me," (Philippians 4:13).
> Godly affirmation: "I can tackle daunting tasks because my God gives me the strength and wisdom to do so. Getting started is the hardest part so I will do five minutes."

One more example:
> Negative self-centered inner voice: "I don't belong or fit in. I am worthless. I am no good."
> Prayer: Lord, help me see myself as you see me, precious and of value.
> Scripture: "For you created my innermost being, you knit me together in my mother's womb. I praise you because I am fearfully and wonderfully made," (Psalm 139: 13-14).

> Godly affirmation: "I am of great worth, precious and valuable to the God of the Universe. He created me, loves me and has appointed my days."

Even though the affirmation may not feel accurate in your life, speak it out loud as truth. For, Gods word is true no matter what you currently "feel". Remember, you are rewriting the script in your head.

Write your scripture, and affirmation on a card. Read it aloud every morning, noon and evening. Allow God to speak to your heart and soul, to retrain your subconscious, replacing your previous self-centered negative thinking with constructive thoughts. If negative patterns interfere with your quiet contemplation on God's truth, tell yourself, "Thank you, self, for bringing that up, but from now on I choose to contemplate on Gods best for me." In time, new mind tapes will replace destructive old tapes. A slow, quiet change will take place in your subconscious that sets you free from the chains of old strongholds through the power of God's word. Try it for six months or longer, every day. You will love the results.

Caution don't mistake this for the "name it and claim it" philosophy whereby you declare you will get a new Porsche and it comes about. A quiet time of mediation based upon the word of God sheds the old nature and cultivates a sound mind. Big difference. Whatever you do, bathe it in prayer and guidance from the Lord.

> Trust in the Lord with all your heart and lean not on your own understanding; in all your ways submit to him, and he will make your paths straight.
>
> (Proverbs 3:5–6)

As you experience rejuvenated self-talk in one aspect, move onto another as the Lord guides. Be diligent and you will see profound differences in your life.

> Our God is an awesome God. He will make us new if we let him, if we believe him and follow his directions. Ready for breakfast? Let's see, powdered eggs and dried cheese. Yum!

Prayer: Father God, our minds are so stuck in ruts, like a car stuck in the mud with wheels spinning even deeper. We need a board stuck under the wheel to provide traction. Show each of us a custom exit ramp to change our subconscious thought patterns. Renew our mind, O Lord. Amen.

Hide in My Heart: If anyone is in Christ, he is a new creation; the old has gone, the new has come (2 Corinthians 5:17).

Choose Today: I am new in Christ. He is renewing my mind from deep within my being.

Week 27, Day 2. Read: Romans 12:2.

Action Tool: Here is a quick exercise to understand how powerful God made your *thoughts* in shaping your outlook. Read through the entire exercise first, then close your eyes and think.

- ❖ Sit quietly. Visualize a pleasant scene in nature. Notice how you feel. Consider your physical body–your head, heart, stomach. How do they feel?
- ❖ Now shift your thoughts to some troubling, depressing situation. Really get into it. Dwell on a serious worry. Note how you feel now. Notice any physical changes in your body. Do you feel a sense of weight pressing upon you? Consider your physical body–your head, heart, stomach. How do they feel?
- ❖ Now eyes up! Lift your thoughts to God. Toss your trouble into His hands; He who throws them into the sea. Take a deep breath. Affirm, "I have cast my cares upon God for He cares for me." Inventory how you feel. What about your energy level? Your stomach, head, heart? Assuredly, your spirit lifted. This a more wholesome place to dwell (live-in) as you face the hardships of life.

Journal: Describe your experience during the exercise.

Week 27, Day 3. Read: Psalm 139.
Journal: How was your makeup formed as God wove it together in your mother's womb? Once leaving the safety of that gentle environment what cruel stresses bombarded you to form your inner self-image?
Action Tool: Create a "Pattern for Renewing Your Mind" for your specific rut of negative thinking. Remember the affirmation may not be true *now*, even so, write it from the viewpoint of how God sees you. Pattern for Renewing Your Mind:

Negative inner voice:

Prayer:

Scripture:

Godly affirmation:

Week 27, Day 4. Read: James 1:12–18, 4:1–8.
Journal: What is your inner voice dictating about your daily reaction to life? How is this inner voice in direct opposition to the voice of God?
Action Tool: Read aloud your "Pattern for Renewing Your Mind" created yesterday. Sit quietly and affirm deep within that your Father God is transforming you.

Week 27, Day 5. Read: James 1:17–18, 3:12–18.
Journal: Ask the Lord to reveal the ruts, the habitual thinking patterns, which bring you down and encourage defeat. Pray for insight regarding scriptures and affirmations will work together with the Holy Spirit to renew your mind.
Action Tool: Read aloud the "Pattern of Renewing Your Mind".

Lumbering Black Bear
Week 28, Day 1

Better a woman meets a bear robbed of her cubs than a fool bent on folly.

(Proverbs 17:12)

> Ladies, over there, a bear! A black bear lumbering along through the forest! Make noise, yell, and clap your hands. Fun to see but not too close! Bears, even strolling bears, become dangerous if they think we have food or move between Mama bear and her cubs.

Just as an unexpected bear may come plodding along the trail, so can worry, doubts, and anxiety, stroll into your life during a typical day. We need to be alert, to clap, yell, do whatever, to send the potentially dangerous emotional intruder on his way.

As is frequent for me, I awoke with trouble on my mind. Worries steeped and cycled. Knowing from long practice and God's instruction, exactly what to do, I gave each concern over to God. I surrendered my family to One who can save and transform.

By the time my brain was fully engaged I was silently singing, "Today is the day the Lord hath make; I will rejoice and be glad in it." Hot tea in hand, still in pajamas, God and I met in my private corner where I sat for a moment just staring out the window. "Lord, guide my day. Show me what is meaningful amidst the routine. Often, it all seems so pointless and repetitive. Grant me your gift of gladness of heart and satisfaction in my work today."

My quiet moments are often brief, then off I rush. Occasionally, time grants a gracious hour. Encouraged and refreshed by the word of God, I sought my Honey Bear Husband for morning hugs. Though grey and rainy outside, sun shone in my heart. God had control over the lives of my loved ones, so I left it with Him (at least for the moment).

Starting victorious, however, does not mean ending it so. Countless times I have exited my prayer corner, rejoicing, to have an immediate fight with my husband or issue with my children or a daunting task. Almost every single afternoon my spirits dive. Let's examine the lumbering bear named "Slump." Slump tempts women to wallowing in discouragement and self-pity. Lord Help!

Here are the most common factors that start the downward spiral:

- ❖ Fatigue and low blood sugar.
- ❖ Inability to tackle an overwhelming task.
- ❖ Unpleasant words with someone important to you.
- ❖ Clutching your troubles and worry to your breast.
- ❖ Bad habit of destructive self-talk.

Our heart cries out again,

> How long O Lord? Will you forget me forever? How long will you hide your face from me? How long must I wrestle with my thoughts and every day have sorrow in my heart?
> (Psalm 13:1–2a)

Still, if we look up and remember Him, he speaks encouragement, yet again,

> You, my daughter, in all these things we are more than conquerors through him who loved us.
> (Romans 8:37)

Then He reminds us,

> For the Word of God is living and active. Sharper than any double-edges sword, it penetrates even to dividing soul and spirit, joints and marrow; it judges the thoughts and attitudes of the heart.
> (Hebrews 4:12–13)

Therefore, He has provided the tools to overcome this daily emotional dive; to do the NEXT RIGHT THING. God is with you and will help you if you but take one step in the right direction. Only a fool ignores a bear coming their way. Better to apply scripture and get a grip on your downward spiral; your bear named Slump.

While shopping in a thrift shop, discouragement suddenly overwhelmed me. My worry from the morning, descended upon me again with fruitless, self-incriminating thoughts. However, when Slump threatened to ruin my attitude, I implemented the Stop Cure (see the action tools). Outwardly, I kept looking at stuff, but inwardly I prayed, recited scripture and praised God. If anyone noticed, a woman was considering a blouse. No special event. Yet for me, inside, victory in Jesus. With God's grace, Slump defeated! If I can do it, so can you!

> That was exciting, seeing a bear! Once, as a young woman of twenty-one, I ventured backpacking alone. Foolish me. That night I was asleep on my tummy in my bag without a tent when a bear cub walked across my back! Well, I made a noise all right, screaming and yelling, scaring the cub away. Thinking about the mama bear, I grabbed my whistle, pot and spoon laid near the head of my bed. I blew and banged for a considerable time. The cub and mama bear wandered away. Thank God.

Prayer: Lord, in the moment of everyday life, we forget to turn to you, especially during "slump" times. Seal scripture in our minds and bring it to the forefront when we need to fight off the daily slump. Thank you for victory through Christ Jesus. Amen.

Hide in My Heart: "For I am more than a conqueror through him who loves me," (Romans 8:37).

Choose Today: I have victory because of Jesus even over the afternoon slump!

Week 28, Day 2. Read: Psalm 13:1–2a.

Journal: What specific time of day you often feel discouraged and depressed. Now consider how your mind spirals downward. What thinking ignites and fuels this lumbering bear?

Action Tool: Stop Cure
    STOP! (Remember a stop sign.)
    U-TURN. If negative self-talk sneaks in, say to yourself, "Thank you self, but I prefer to trust in the Lord."
    EYES UP! Pray and praise.

Week 28, Day 3. Read: Hebrews 4:12–13.
Journal: Pray for a verse that will set your eyes on Him. Record the scripture you find to counteract this slump. (Tip: Pick a word that relates to your downward thoughts. Search the Bible index for related verses.)
Action Tool: Build endorphins (feel-good hormones) by taking a brisk 10-minute walk.

Week 28, Day 4. Read: Proverbs 17:12.
Journal: Consider whether your slump is due to a physical issue. Educate yourself on what to do for fatigue, high or low blood sugar, etc. especially when life is stressful. Record what you find.
Action Tool: PROTEIN SNACK. Notice a routine fatigue that appears emotional but is physical. Have a healthy snack handy; praise God while savoring it.

Week 28, Day 5. Read: Romans 8:37.
Journal: Consider whether the slump is due to feelings of being overwhelmed. How can this be countered with healthy thinking and actions?
Action Tool: FIVE MINUTE RULE. If it is a task that is daunting you, tell yourself 5 minutes is all you need to give it, and then you are free.

Thorny Bushes
Week 29, Day 1

A gentle answer turns away wrath, but a harsh word stirs up anger.

(Proverbs 15:1)

> My life is an open book to you now, fellow journey friends. That being so, would you like to hear a little story I wrote back when my children were elementary school age and my journey full-on intense with desperation? Ok, I thought you would. Settle on a patch of grass and make yourself a mocha with my portable expresso machine while I dig the story out of my backpack.

"Something's Gotta' Change"

Lucy kicked her sister's new soccer ball into the ball-eating bushes. Daddy would remove the bushes someday and find the balls. But for now, those bushes were so thick and thorny that once a ball landed in the ball-eating bushes, no one ever saw it again.

"I never want to play with you again," yelled Lily. "Mom, she kicked my new soccer ball into the bushes on purpose."

"I didn't!" pouted Lucy. "I didn't mean to."

"Yes, you did, you cotton-head."

Mom stared at a complex recipe as the twins ran into the kitchen. Flowers and good china graced the table set for company. Clutter covered the living room. Unprepared dishes of vegetables and chicken occupied the counters. Mom grimaced with frustration. "Go Away!" she snapped, "I'm busy. Go to your rooms. Now!" Mom reached for salt and knocked the container of flour on the floor. "Awgh! One more interruption and you can cook dinner!

Lily and Lucy grinned, "Sure." Lucy pushed Lily, "It's my turn to help with dinner."

"It is not!" said Lily as she opened the cupboard to look for a cookie. "You did it last time."

Mom, wiping the flour off the floor, stood up quickly banging her head on the cupboard. "Out, out, out. I can't stand it. Get out of here and stop arguing!"

She grabbed each girl by the shirt and marched them to their rooms, slamming the doors. A few minutes later a scowling Dad, walked in from work. "He did it again. Jim undermines my work. He makes me furious! I don't know how I can continue working with him."

Big brother, Josh, wandered out of his room. "Mom, when will you get my patches sewn on my ranger shirt? I need it tomorrow."

Dad glared at Josh, "I am talking with your mother. You are interrupting! Well, go ahead. What is so important?"

Josh sighed, "Nothing Dad, it can wait." As he returned to his room, anger churned. He closed his door and plunged into a computer game.

Dad turned to Mom, "If something doesn't change…"

"I'm not listening," declared Mom. "The Hardwick's and MacDuff's arrive in half an hour."

"Ok, ok," grumbled Dad. Heading towards the couch, he noticed junk strewn over the living room. "Girls get in here right this minute and clean up this mess. You know we have company coming. Such little piggies!"

At dinner Dad, Mom, Josh, Lily, Lucy, the Hardwick's and MacDuff's bowed their heads for grace. "Lord God, we thank you for our friends and this good food, for being our Savior and blessing us with your love. Amen."

All evening, as the families talked and laughed together, Mom kept thinking, "If something doesn't change… if something doesn't change…"

> My girls got a kick out of this little story. They thought it funny, but I didn't. My earnest prayers cried out, "Change us Lord." Ok, packs on, ladies, today we climb Treachery Pass and Over the Cliff of Anger. We better strengthen up with prayer. Lord….

Prayer: Lord, all those angry words are not for good. We spew them out of frustration. Lord change us! Teach us to respond to anger with a gentle answer. Start with me, Lord, start with me. Amen.

Hide in My Heart: "A gentle answer turns away wrath, but a harsh word stirs up anger," (Proverbs 15:1).

Choose Today: Through the power of God, I choose to not sin in my anger.

Week 29, Day 2. Read: Proverbs 29:11.
Action Tool: Just for Today
Tackling a new thought pattern for a lifetime is a daunting task. Therefore, choose one of the 10 scriptural based changes to work on "Just for Today".

- *Just for today*, I will give thanks despite all circumstances, difficulties, bad luck or angry people. (Based on 1 Thessalonians 5:18)
- *Just for today*, I will release my need to be in control and/or to fix what is broken. I will let God take over. (Based on Proverbs 3:5–6)
- *Just for today*, I will lift my hands to the heavens, release my anxious thoughts to Jesus who will fling them into the sea. (Based on Psalm 139: 23–24)
- *Just for today*, I will set my focus ahead, not backward, knowing "God is with me today." He is working through my past circumstances to transform me and bring about good. (Based on 2 Corinthians 5:17)
- *Just for today*, I will choose one family member to shower with encouragement, praise and love in action. (Based on Ephesians 4:29)
- *Just for today*, I will ask for and receive God's gift of gladness of heart. I choose joy. (Based on Ecclesiastes 5:20)
- *Just for today*, I will do something nice for someone in secret. (Based on John 13:34–35)
- *Just for today*, I will not complain. When I discover myself complaining, I will say to myself, "Thank you for your comments, but today, instead of being upset, I will be thankful for what is good." (Based on Philippians 2:14)

- ❖ *Just for today,* I will forgive anyone who hurts me, even when they are unrepentant, by the strength of the Holy Spirit within me. (Based on Matthew 18:21–22)

Journal: Choose one "Just for Today". Write it in your journal. Focus on this effort for today.

Week 29, Day 3. Read: James 1:19–20.
Journal: Journal how well you acted on yesterday's choice. If you failed, begin again. View today as a new day! Choose one "Just for Today".
Action Tool: Just for Today

Week 29, Day 4. Read: Proverbs 15:1.
Journal: Journal how well you acted on yesterday's choice. If you failed, begin again. View today as a new day! Choose one "Just for Today".
Action Tool: Just for Today

Week 29 Day 5. Read: Psalm 25:4–5.
Journal: Journal how well you acted on yesterday's choice. If you failed, begin again. View today as a new day! Choose one "Just for Today".
Action Tool: Continue "Just for Today" until you have completed the list. Repeat.

Treachery Pass
Week 30, Day 1

> **An angry man (woman) stirs up conflict, and a hot-tempered man (woman) commits many sins.**
> **(Proverbs 29:22)**

> Gals be courageous. The trail narrows along Treachery Pass with a high wall of rock on our right and a steep drop off on our left. One false move threatens a plunge to death. Cling to the wall; use your staff as a third leg to balance. Lord, protect us.

An anger grenade hides in every mind. Ignited, this grenade devastates relationships. For some, anger is close to the surface. Our mouth spews stinging words and accusations. For others, antagonism brews deep seeping out in sneaky passive-aggressive sabotage. Some people bury fury in stomach pain or manifest bitterness through depression. Like a fire out of control, unleashed anger destroys.

I hear you proclaim, "Jesus got angry. God is jealous, wrathful, and exercises vengeance." Yes, sin and injustice provoke God the Father to anger. Yet in His passionate response our God and his son Jesus remain holy, filled with love and forgiveness, sound in judgment. He remains constant. Our nature, unlike God, lives in continual conflict between good and evil. As a result, we have difficulty responding to emotional situations without sinning.

Instead, we grasp anger close to our heart. Human nature nurtures and embellishes animosity. Using outrage as a weapon to bludgeon is a normal human response. We believe our mad punishes him or her. Desire to guarantee our own way fuels the antagonism. Our reasoning justifies resentment. The evil one approves and encourages this response. Do you really want this?

The emotion of anger is not sin. Anger is a flashing signal indicating something is wrong and needs fixing. Outrage can motivate constructive action within our self, our relationships, or our society. This is righteous anger.

> In your anger do not sin: Do not let the sun go down while you are still angry.
> (Ephesians 4:26)

To "be angry and sin not" you must obey God's word with no exceptions, following the example of God and Jesus.

> But just as he who called you is holy, so be holy *in all you do*: for it is written: Be holy, because I am Holy.
> (1 Peter 1:15)

The results of harboring sinful anger:

- **Sabotages righteousness** – The anger of man (woman) does not bring about the righteousness of God. (James 1:20)
- **Causes strife** – A hot-tempered man (woman) stirs up dissensions, but a patient man (woman) calms a quarrel. (Proverbs 15:18)
- **Devastates those around** – Anger is cruel and fury overwhelming and who can stand before jealousy. (Proverbs 27:4)
- **Is dwelling in sin** – The acts of the sinful nature are obvious: hatred, discord, jealousy, fits of rage, selfish ambition, dissensions, factions and the like. (Galatians 5:19)
- **Causes you to be a fool** – A fool gives full vent to his anger, but a wise man keeps himself under control. (Proverbs 29:11)
- **Prevents Understanding** – A patient man has great understanding, but a quick-tempered man displays folly. (Proverbs 14:29)
- **Leads to more sin** – An angry man stirs up dissension, and a hot-tempered man must pay the penalty; if you rescue him, you will have to do it again. (Proverbs 29:22)
- **Causes isolation as others avoid you** – Do not make friends with a hot-tempered man, do not associate with one easily angered,

or you may learn his ways and get yourself ensnared. (Proverbs 22:24–25)
- ❖ **Reduces the ability to lead** – An overseer is entrusted with God's work, he must not be overbearing, quick-tempered but self-controlled, and disciplined. (Titus 1:7)
- ❖ **Makes one unbearable to live with** – Better to live on a corner of the roof, then share a house with a quarrelsome wife (husband). (Proverbs 21:9)

Unbridled anger accelerates a fall to death; death of trust, love, a relationship, etc. It is time, today, to cleanse harbored malice. Old warehouses of bitterness from years past impact our life. Stored animosity causes quick tempers and ill health. By harboring anger, the one with whom we are angry controls us.

God instructs us,

> Get rid of all bitterness, rage and anger, brawling and slander, along with every form of malice.
> (Ephesians 4:31)

Since God requires elimination of these qualities, he will enable us to overcome them. But how? Hold on until next week. For now, perceiving the need for change is enough.

> I am so glad Treachery Pass is behind us, still up ahead, the Cliffs of Anger. Oh my! Sisters, I never even knew I was angry until God revealed it. He opened festering wounds. It hurt so much but healing began. It was a long inner journey from bitterness to peace.

Prayer: God Almighty, will the pain of being such a wretch never end? I am so tired of how little I measure up to your standards; I feel like giving up. I have no control over my anger. It happens then seeps out. Help! And my Father said, "I know, daughter. I sent my son to rescue you. I am your help."

Hide in My Heart: "Show me your ways, O Lord, teach me your paths; guide me in your truth and teach me, for you are God my Savior and my hope is in you all the day long." (Psalms 25:4–5).
Choose Today: I am willing, Lord, to look at my anger and deal with it. Start with me today.

Week 30, Day 2. Read: Proverbs 29:22 and Ephesians 4:31.
Journal: Pray for a willingness to see your anger as God sees it. Ask for His strength to tackle this stronghold in your life. Journal these prayers and His response.
Action Tool:
>STOP! Use the hand signal when anger rises.
>U-TURN! Turn yourself around to reset your mind.
>PRAY! Ask God to convict and guide you.

Week 30, Day 3. Read: 1 Peter 1:15–16 and Psalms 25:4–5.
Journal: Which action on the following list is characteristic of you? Explosion, beating a pillow, stuffing, exercise, yelling, throwing, seethe, verbal attack, talk-talk-talk, deny, justify, blame others or circumstances. What are the festering wounds in your life causing you to "sin in your anger"?
Action Tool: U-TURN. Think of a common circumstance that triggers instant anger for you. Now think STOP, U-TURN. Turn around or make a U-turn motion with your finger. Pray.

Week 30, Day 4. Read: Reread the *"results of harboring anger"*.
Journal: What evidence of harboring anger do you see in your life. Ask God to help you to let go of your "claim" to have a right to be angry.
Action Tool: PRACTICE today in your mind. STOP, U-TURN, PRAY.

Week 30, Day 5. Memorize and Act on Scripture
Read: James 1:19–22.
Journal: Write today's verse in your journal. Write this week's memory verse in your journal also, making it a prayer of your heart.
Action Tool: Practice. STOP, U-TURN, PRAY.

Cliffs of Anger
Week 31, Day 1

> **We also rejoice in our sufferings, because we know that suffering produces perseverance, perseverance, character and character, hope, and hope does not disappoint us, because God has poured out his love into our hearts by the Holy Spirit, whom he has given us.**
> **(Romans 5:3-5)**

> This is an embarrassing story. Is it ok, Monica, if I tell it?" We returned home after a lovely family outing. Little Monica scampered into the house. Back outside she curled in my lap cooing, "Mommy, I love you." A little while later, I found Monica had dumped my jewelry out the window, cut up my bedspread, and defecated on the bed. I was furious. I marched outside, grabbed her collar, pulled her into the bedroom and put her face to the pooh. Horrified, I burst into uncontrollable tears. I washed her face, put her in her room and ran into the backyard crying, angry at God, Monica, and myself.

Hope. I had lost hope. Thinking it depended on me, I was beyond myself with how to bring my family healing. Four-year-old Monica was just acting out the pain of her early years in the orphanage. A moment of fury hurled me, the "Godly Christian Adult", out of control. Me, the calm one in the family! So, what hope?

First, getting rid of anger and bitterness depends on a heart change, no other way will work. You must yearn to put off anger and allow God to work in you. It requires wholehearted obedience to God's, even if your feelings dictate otherwise. An impossible goal without trust in God's reliability.

> We also rejoice in our sufferings, because we know that suffering produces perseverance, perseverance, character: and character, hope, and hope does not disappoint us, because God has poured out his love into our hearts by the Holy Spirit whom he has given us.
>
> (Romans 5:3-5)

I did not want this suffering. Given the circumstances, frustration and indignation were natural.

Nevertheless, anger did not harvest good results. But what could I do? Since the emotion of anger is not sin, what is?

- ❖ Outbursts, discord, rage. (Galatians 5:20)
- ❖ When not accompanied by compassion. (Psalm 86:15)
- ❖ When not accompanied by forgiveness. (Romans 12:17)
- ❖ When it violates Biblical Love. (1 Corinthians 13:1–13)
- ❖ When it causes you to speak words that are not uplifting. (Ephesians 4:29)
- ❖ When the sun goes down on your anger. (Ephesians 4:26)
- ❖ When it does not bring honor to God. (1 Corinthians 10:31)
- ❖ When it causes you to neglect praying, giving thanks to God, or rejoicing. (1 Thessalonians 5:16–17)

Anger is sinful when it causes you to violate these scriptures:
- ❖ Bless those who persecute you. (Romans 12:14)
- ❖ Obey the authorities. (Romans 13:1–5)
- ❖ Trust God and be content. (1 Timothy 6:6)
- ❖ Restore people gently. (Galatians 6:1)
- ❖ Not provoke your children. (Ephesians 6:4)

Our human nature demands our way, our wants, our needs, our rights, our obsession for no strife or pain. Others must "pay" for upsetting our day. Children must "feel our fury" for successful discipline.

> What causes fights and quarrels among you? Don't they come from your desires that battle within you? You want something but don't get it. You kill and covet, but you cannot have what you want. You quarrel and flight. You do not have because you do not ask God. When you ask, you do not receive, because you ask with wrong motives.
>
> (James 4:1-3a)

Our bitterness shows despair at God's plan for our daily circumstances and a lack of understanding of God's purpose for anger. This seething leads to evil. Remember the story of Cain and Able? One brother killed the other because of his jealousy. Amid incidents that ignite our anger (interfere, irritate), we are to bless the people who hurt us. He gives power for this supernatural behavior as we yield to Him.

> Do not repay evil with evil or insult with insult, but with blessing because to this you were called so that you may inherit a blessing.
>
> (1 Peter 3:9)

Pay attention to the promise, "that I might inherit a blessing". If I desire the blessing, I must be obedient.

> Consider it pure joy, my brother, whenever you face trials of many kinds, because you know that the testing of your faith develops perseverance. Perseverance must finish its work that you may be mature, and complete not lacking anything.
>
> (James 1:2–4)

We say, "I have my rights! They have wronged me." God comforts, "I understand. I will work it for good if you trust me. Follow my way. Stick to my game plan."

> Oh, Monica, will you forgive me for being such a failure? The Godly response instructs, yes, be angry (who wouldn't be). Yet, step aside, consider my actions before responding. View my fury as a warning signal. Act in compassion, prayer and appropriate discipline resulting in God's blessing. Wish I could run the clock back. Not possible, so I press on learning to react with the love of God.

Prayer: Here we are again, Lord, on the Cliffs of Anger, unwilling and unable to change our automatic angry reactions. Help, O God. I claim your victory in this arena of my life. Lord, open my eyes to judge myself first. Amen.

Hide in My Heart: "First take the log out of your own eye, then you will see clearly to remove the speck from your brother's eye" (Matthew 7:5).

Choose Today: Today, I choose to view anger your way, opening myself to your correction.

Week 31, Day 2. Read: Matthew 7:5.

Journal: Take a recent circumstance which ignited your anger. Judge yourself. Describe a Biblical response to the same circumstance?

Action Tool: Look back at the verses on "sinful anger" from today's lesson. Circle the ones that convict you.

Week 31, Day 3. Seek His Guidance

Read: Romans 5:3–5.

Journal: How has being provoked to anger resulted in lost hope? How will responding God's way bring hope again?

Action Tool: "Practice a Godly Response" by applying the below steps to an anger-provoking situation.

> JUDGE SELF FIRST – Stand still and look within instead of out. What could I have done differently?
> FORGIVE – Do I want the healing of forgiveness? Then I must forgive.
> BLESS – If I bless, the other, then I will be blessed. Do I want a blessing?

Week 31, Day 4. Read: 1 Peter 3:9.
Journal: How can you bless someone with whom you are angry.
Action Tool: Repeat yesterday's exercise.

Week 31, Day 5. Read: James 1:2–4.
Journal: This scripture is counter intuitive. It goes against our human nature. Obviously, God is not calling us to be happy, happy in the face of trials. What does this scripture mean to you and how can you apply his words of encouragement?
Action Tool: Repeat once again "Practice a Godly Response".

Abba's Trail
Week 32, Day 1

> **In your anger do not sin; do not let the sun go down while you are still angry, and do not give the devil a foothold.**
>
> **(Ephesians 4:26–27)**

> Careful, adventurous ones! Peek over these sheer granite cliffs. Down yonder camp awaits. Goodness! The trail disappeared. This mountain of granite shows no evidence of previous hikers. No way this old lady will rappel down. Look! Over there, a little pile of stones. A cairn, rocks piled one upon another, mark the way. Let's take it. Through the bushes, girls. Wait! Here is an old wooden sign on the ground saying, "Abba's Trail".

How, how, how does one remember, in the moment of anger, to response as God would have us respond? In fact, what is a righteous response? Is God saying to swallow frustrations and let people walk all over us? What if the circumstances justify our angry? Our common response goes:

- ❖ Nothing will change if I give up my anger.
- ❖ I am right. I deserve to be mad.
- ❖ He/She needs to change, not me.
- ❖ Outrage intimidates and gets action. It works for me.
- ❖ Easier said than done, letting go of anger when nothing has changed. Not worth it.

When circumstances incite anger, you have a serious choice:

Focus on Our Own Way = chaos, fragmentation, separation, sorrow and death.

Focus on God's Way = peace, joy, and wholeness and oneness.

Shall we jump off the cliff or follow Abba's Trail (Abba = Daddy)? As you walk His trail, anger subsides, and restoration of the relationship begins. It isn't easy or quick, but worth the journey. God gave us the choice. Reap the destruction of our selfish nature or the wholeness of God's way.

During raising my "Angry Family" my husband was verbally explosive, son stowed pain, and daughter sabotaged goodness. Plus, throw in me caring for dying parents and the hormonal changes of menopause. My stress level was off the wall causing chronic fatigue. Being passive-aggressive, I seethed. Calmness amid turmoil? Impossible.

In response to my plea, through a study of the scriptures, God guided me to *"The Mad to Glad Pathway"*. Made up of reminder words and scriptures, the pathway leads from anger to restoration. Posted on my wall, tucked in my purse, stuck on my car visor, used as a bookmark, the pathway card anchored my attention. When upset, I sat in a quiet corner alone or walked around the block working through *Mad to Glad*. Mommy on time out! This process enabled me to deal with the situation in a Godly manner.

Mad to Glad Pathway
God's Direction for How to Respond When Angry

1. <u>STOP</u> Be quick to listen, slow to speak, and slow to become angry. (James 1:19)
2. <u>THINK</u> (TEST OR TEMPTATION) Be self-controlled and alert. Your enemy the devil prowls around like a roaring lion looking for someone to devour. Resist him, standing firm in the faith. (1 Peter 5:8–9) All things work together for good for those who love the Lord and are called according to his purpose. For those he foreknew he also predestined to be conformed to the image of God, that they might be the firstborn among many brethren. (Romans 8:28–29)
3. <u>PRAY</u> Do not be anxious about anything but with prayer and petition present your requests to God, and the peace of God which

surpasses all understanding will guard your heart and mind in Christ Jesus. (Philippians 4:6–7)

4. <u>U-TURN</u> Do not conform to the pattern of this world but be transformed by the renewing of your mind. Then you will be able to test and approve what God's will is—his good, pleasing and perfect will. (Romans 12:2)
5. <u>JUDGE SELF</u> First take the log out of your own eye, then you will see clearly to remove the speck from your brother's eye. (Matthew 7:5)
6. <u>FORGIVE</u> Then Peter came to Jesus and asked, "Lord, how many times shall I forgive my brother or sister who sins against me? Up to seven times?" Jesus answered, "I tell you, not seven times, but seventy-seven times." (Matthew 18:21–22)
7. <u>BLESS</u> Do not repay evil with evil or insult with insult, but with blessing, because to this you were called so that you may inherit a blessing. (1 Peter 3:9)
8. <u>SPEAK IN LOVE</u> Do not let any unwholesome talk come out of your mouths, but only what is helpful for building others up according to their needs, that it may benefit those who listen. (Ephesians 4:29)
9. <u>RESTORE GENTLY</u> Brothers if someone is caught in a sin you who are spiritual should restore him gently. But watch yourself, or you also may be tempted. (Galatian 6:1)

So, let's bring it home by taking an imaginary "Time-Out Walk" to see the thinking process of applying "Mad to Glad". God's word instructs you to take control of your anger and bring about restoration. Therefore, since He works in us, it is possible if we are willing.

> Angry? Walk… Huff, huff, huff with scripture.
> STOP. Just do it! (Stop Sign with your hand.)
> THINK? Test or Temptation? Blessings or Chaos? Do I want God's blessings or my own chaos resulting in victory for the evil one?
> PRAY. Ask God for help and wisdom.

U-TURN. Turn around, repent, go in God's direction. (Physically, turn your body around or make a circle with your finger to symbolize turning around.)

JUDGE SELF. What could I have done different? What is my responsibility in this situation? What signal for change needed is the anger revealing?

FORGIVE. For my own healing, I must forgive the other person involved, even if the other person hasn't changed or apologized. Am I willing? Ask God to enable you to forgive.

BLESS. What can I do to bless the person with whom I am angry? Bathe him/her in prayer. Seek a sincere way to bless.

SPEAK IN LOVE. Not in anger. Am I ready to speak with love? What words will benefit? How can I speak the truth about my feelings and the situation, even about the other person's responsibility without being spiteful?

RESTORE GENTLY. Now you are ready to talk with a gentle and quiet spirit.

> Abba's means Daddy, so we hiked Daddy's Trail. Strenuous trek, wasn't it, gals? Tonight, we camp beside a crystal-clear mountain lake; God's blessing for traversing this difficult path to faithful dealing with anger.

Prayer: Lord, open our brains to absorb your scriptures, so we remember when the moment of testing comes. Give us hearts overwhelmingly motivated to choose wholeness over chaos. Amen.

Hide in My Heart: *Mad to Glad Pathway.*

Choose Today: I choose to serve you, my God, even when I am angry.

Week 32, Day 2. Read: Ephesians 4:26.
Journal: Ask God to reveal your anger the instant it emerges. How do you express anger? Instant, controlled, slow simmering, rage, passive aggressive, swallowing it? How are you sinning in your anger?
Action Tool: Print out and laminate the *Mad to Glad Pathway* from this week's lesson. Tuck copies in convenient places for easy access when needed. Memorize the steppingstones: STOP, THINK, PRAY, U-TURN, JUDGE SELF, FORGIVE, BLESS, SPEAK IN LOVE, RESTORE GENTLY. Practice until you can recite it instantly.

Week 32, Day 3. Read: *Mad to Glad Pathway.*
Journal: What steps in the *Mad to Glad Pathway* are the hardest for you? Describe your current reactions. With prayer, outline an alternate reaction following scripture guidelines.
Action Tool: Memorizing the steppingstones. Work on memorizing the scriptures.

Week 32, Day 4. Read: *Mad to Glad Pathway.*
Journal: How can you bless someone when you are still angry with them and they are unrepentant? What spiritually and physically can you do to bless him/her? How is blessing different from allowing abuse? Ask the Lord for insight?
Action Tool: Continue memorizing *Mad to Glad Pathway.*

Week 32, Day 5. Read: *Mad to Glad Pathway.*
Journal: Instead of lashing out or swallowing our anger, we are to speak the truth in love and restore gently. How do we do this if the other person picks up the argument where it left off? How do we avoid slipping back into sin in our anger? Ask the Lord for guidance for your own situation.
Action Tool: Continue memorizing *Mad to Glad Pathway.*

Serenity Lake
Week 33, Day 1

Do not repay evil with evil or insult with insult, but with blessing, because to this you were called so that you may inherit a blessing.

(1 Peter 3:9)

Ahhh, heavenly to shed our packs and lounge, gazing upon the stunning view of Serenity Lake framed by the towering Cliffs of Anger. Wow, we did it, girls. We hiked to camp from that granite precipice. Good for us!

Because dealing with anger according to scripture is so important, please listen in while the Holy Spirit confronts me in a true-life incident.

<u>Anne</u>: "I am so angry. Do you know what my husband did? Yea, that's what he did. I am so mad that I can hardly see straight. Forgiveness? No way! I am going to, urrr... I don't know what I will do! He hurt me so bad. He is so wrong."

<u>Holy Spirit</u>: "Anne, STOP!"

<u>Anne</u>: "No! Applying scripture to this incident is not an option. He's not even sorry. If I don't make sure he knows how wrong he is, how bad he's hurt me, he'll just keep on doing this. And I will not stand for it!"

<u>Holy Spirit</u>: "Anne, Stop! Be quick to listen, slow to speak, and slow to become angry. For the anger of a man, woman, boy or girl, does not bring about the righteousness of God."

<u>Anne</u>: "Well, right now, I don't want God's righteousness. I want to explode. Why do I have to hurt like this? It's not fair."

<u>Holy Spirit:</u> "Anne, STOP. THINK. For all things work together for good for those who love the Lord and are called according to his purpose and do not repay evil for evil but with blessing." Do you want

this argument to prompt evil, pain and suffering or insight and healing? Your choice."

Anne: "No way this could work together for good. Absolutely, no way."

Holy Spirit: "Is God's word lying? Or is it truth? Do you believe or not?"

Anne: "OK, I believe. I'll apply scripture out of obedience to you, God. But in truth, I prefer harboring my animosity a while longer."

Holy Spirit: "THINK TEST or TEMPTATION. For those he foreknew he also predestined to be conformed to the image of Christ so that they may be the firstborn among many brethren. If you yield to God, Anne, He can use this to develop patience, strength, and love in you. This moment of pain will mold you in Christlikeness. Blessings will result. If you do not yield to God, you will be allowing Satan to influence you. The evil one encourages anger as an excuse to sin. The natural consequences of sin intensify sorrow and death. No blessings.

Anne: "Alright, I prefer your blessings, Lord, and I certainly don't want more sorrow. What now?"

Holy Spirit: PRAY. "Do not be anxious about anything but in everything with prayer and petition present your requests to God, and the peace of God which transcends all understanding will guard your heart and mind in Christ Jesus."

Anne: "Lord, I'm so mad, please transform my heart and enable me to let go of my anger."

Holy Spirit: "U-TURN. Set your heart to go in God's direction. Do not conform to the pattern of this world but be transformed by the renewing of your mind. Then you will be able to test and approve what God's will is—his good, pleasing and perfect will."

Anne: "Ok, I am turning around. I'd better turn around again. One more time. Ok, I am ready. What's next?"

Holy Spirit: "JUDGE SELF FIRST, Anne. Now, take the log out of your own eye, then you will see clearly to remove the speck from your husband's eye."

Anne: "But you don't understand, my husband was the wrong one here."

Holy Spirit: "Anne, your husband's error will overpower your discernment regarding the argument until you judge yourself."

<u>Anne</u>: "OK, judge self-first. I overreacted. Then spew hurtful words. Unleashed resentments stored up for months. Yelled and stomped out of the house. But he deserved it! He was yelling too."

<u>Holy Spirit</u>: "No blame shifting, Anne. We aren't dealing with your husband just yet; that will come later. We are dealing with your attitude."

<u>Anne</u>: "So, I could have handled the discussion better. When I found myself spiraling down into fury, stepping away was an option. Pause in prayer, also a good choice. Lean on God to resolve the disagreement rather than insist on my opinion. Anger signals something needs fixing. I could have calmly asked him about his frustration resulting in anger. Is that what you want, Lord?"

<u>Holy Spirit</u>: "Yes, good. NOW FORGIVE. Christ forgives you for this and every other incident, Anne. However, you will suffer the natural consequences of a hard heart if you do not forgive Gene."

<u>Anne</u>: "Forgive him? Again? Humm. A hard heart solidifies into a bitter woman. Not appealing. You tell me to forgive seventy times seven, Lord, so give me the strength and power needed. I choose forgiveness even though I don't want to and don't feel like it. Lord, enable my decision to forgive become a reality in my heart. I will do so even if my husband doesn't change a bit.

<u>Holy Spirit</u>: "Anne, the next step is even harder than forgiving, but God requires it of you, BLESS HIM. Do not repay evil for evil or insult with insult, but with blessing, because to this you were called so that you may inherit a blessing."

<u>Anne</u>: Oh, this is above and beyond reasonable. Bless him when I prefer to bash him with ugly words? But I will do it, Lord, because you ask. Give me wisdom, Jesus, and the ability to bless him with love in my heart. Send your love through me, for at this moment I have none. Of course, I can pray for him. "God in heaven, as I am dealing with my anger, move in my husband's heart to show him his own responsibility. Lord, you convict him. My refraining from badgering him with words will be a blessing to him. Draw us back together with forgiveness and love. Bless my Gene by changing me to respond as you direct."

<u>Holy Spirit</u>: "Good start, Anne. Now bless him with actions."

<u>Anne</u>: "Well, I suppose I could cook him his favorite dinner tonight. Yes, I'll do that."

Holy Spirit: "Good idea. Now when he comes home, and you talk about this morning you must SPEAK THE TRUTH IN LOVE. Let no unwholesome words come out of your mouth, but only what is helpful for building others up according to their needs, that it may benefit those who listen."

Anne: "Yes, Lord, with your help, I will guard my tongue, so that even if he is still angry, I will speak the truth in love. What I perceive are my rights, lay at your feet. Thank you for working within me to calm down and let go."

Holy Spirit: "Anne, the final step is to RESTORE GENTLY. If someone is caught in a sin, you who are spiritual should restore him gently, but watch yourself, or you also may be tempted."

Anne: "Understood. Now that I released my self-righteous focus, my husband's actions may be considered. In speaking with him, admit my responsibility in the argument. Tell him my feelings. Suggest gently how we might do better in the future. Then leave his reaction up to up to God. Oh Lord, how can I do this without starting up the whole argument again? Help me act as your woman."

Gene: "Hi, I'm home. I am so sorry…"

Anne: "Me too. I'm sorry. I…"

Gene: "You made pork chops!"

> It is so peaceful when our hearts and minds are cleansed of bitterness and anger. Our rocks of anger thrown into the lake after supper released so much tension. Even though tomorrow brings its own problems, here at Serenity Lake we dwell in the rest of the Lord. Time for a little shut eye. Sweet Dreams, dear ones.

Prayer: Father God, we so dearly want to inherit your blessings. We know our salvation doesn't rest on our obedience, but life is more victorious when we follow you. Enable us, Lord. Amen.

Hide in My Heart: *Mad to Glad Pathway.*

Choose Today: I choose to be a woman who forgives through the power of Jesus within me.

Week 33, Day 2. Read: Review *Mad to Glad Pathway*.
Journal: List those against whom you are holding a grudge. Declare you will forgive with God's help even if they are not repentant.
Action Tool: Practice *Mad to Glad Pathway* for a specific incident.

Week 33, Day 3. Read: Review *Mad to Glad Pathway*.
Journal: Pour out the reasons you have not forgiven those on the list. Journal how your unforgiveness is affecting you. How is it affecting the other person? Ask the Lord to enable you to forgive even if nothing changes in the situation.
Action Tool: Practice *Mad to Glad Pathway* for a specific incident.

Week 33, Day 4. Read: Review *Mad to Glad Pathway*.
Journal: Process through Mad to Glad considering a person you have not yet forgiven. See where it takes you.

Week 33, Day 5. Read: *Mad to Glad Pathway*.
Journal: What does "speak the truth in love" sound like when you open your mouth? Consider your tone of voice? How do you respond when the other person reacts hostile or rejects your thoughts? Think about expressing your feelings and opinions with "I feel/think" messages, versus attacking "You" messages. Ask the Lord to guide you.
Action Tool: Get outside and walk. Take your *Mad to Glad Pathway*, applying it for a specific incident.

Pack Mules
Week 34, Day 1

> **Take off your old self with its practices and put on the new self, which is being renewed in knowledge in the image of its Creator.**
>
> **(Colossians 3:9-10)**

> Ladies wake up. A string of pack mules is headed into camp! Hello there. We trek out this morning if you need this camp site. What, you are here for us? I don't understand. The outfitter sent fresh supplies and will carry out our garbage? Fantastic! Shed old stuff for fresh food, no brainer.

Backpacking in the wilderness requires packing out every item that will not burn to ashes. Experts carry only essentials. Us, ordinary folk, pack ridiculous amounts of unnecessary junk. Every bit adds weight. After one day hiking, we would shed it gladly. Christ teaches, put-off the old nature and put-on new life in Christ. (Based on Colossians 3)

Put Off
Anger, wrath bitterness, quick-temper, dissension, abusive speech, strife, counting wrongs.
Put On
Patience, kindness, humility, bearing with one another, tenderheartedness, forgiveness, encouragement, love and self-control.

> Those who live according to the flesh have their minds set on what the flesh desires; but those who live in accordance with the Spirit have their minds set on what the Spirit desires. The mind governed by the flesh is death, but the mind governed by the Spirit is life and peace. The mind

> governed by the flesh is hostile to God; it does not submit
> to God's law, nor can it do so. Those who are in the realm
> of the flesh cannot please God. You, however, are not in
> the realm of the flesh but are in the realm of the Spirit, if
> indeed the Spirit of God lives in you. And if anyone does
> not have the Spirit of Christ, they do not belong to Christ.
> (Romans 8:5–9)

Even if we feel great about ourselves, we are flawed, needing improvement. As God molded me via the fires of life it hurt. A quiet peace and joy forged by those fires, though not perfect, abides today deep within me. Allow God to create abundant life and peace.

So, lets "Clean House". When a house is empty, we fill it with furniture, people, stuff, dirt, puppies. Every so often, we deep clean and hold a garage sale. Then what happens? More stuff gradually collects, more dirt accumulates. The same happens with our spiritual "inside me" house.

> When an evil spirit comes out of a man (woman), it goes
> through arid places seeking rest and does not find it. Then
> it says, 'I will return to the house I left.' When it arrives, it
> finds the house unoccupied, swept clean and put in order.
> Then it goes and takes with it seven other spirits more
> wicked than itself, and they go in and live there. The final
> condition of that man (woman) is worse than the first.
> (Matthew 12: 43–45)

The Holy Spirit and an evil spirit cannot occupy the same space. Thus, an evil spirit cannot possess a Christian. Even so, apart from God, our self-improvement efforts are inadequate. We work hard at cleaning up our act, but the old habits return. Maybe, we succeed at self-improvement, yet without God it often becomes prideful arrogance. From our pinacol of success we look down on others for their weaknesses. Zing! Not so clean after all.

God provides a solution in Ephesians 4:22-5:20. Take time, right now, to read these verses in your Bible. Note the words "put-off", "put-on".

You were taught, with regard to your former way of life, to *put off* your old self which is being corrupted by its deceitful desires, to be made new in the attitude of your minds; and to *put on* the new self, created to be like God in true righteousness and holiness.

(Ephesians 4:22-24)

Put Off	**Put On**	
Evil desires	Purity	Good fruit
Disorder	Compassion	Impartiality
Greed	Kindness	Sincerity
Envy	Humility	Order
Idolatry	Gentleness	Wholeness
Bitterness	Patience	Sympathy
Anger	Forgiveness	Harmony
Self-pity	Love	Thanksgiving
Rage	Wisdom	Praise
Critical judgment	Hard Work	Mercy
Malice	Reverence	Judge Self
Slander	Truth	
Filthy language	Perseverance	
Lying	Trust	
Laziness	Faith	
Impurity	Love	
Selfish ambition	Hope	
Sexual immorality	Consideration	

And whatever you do, whether in word or deed, do it all in the name of the Lord Jesus, giving thanks to God the Father, through him.

(Colossians 3:17)

> Problem is, I like my stuff! I cherish my stuff, even my emotional stuff. It is so hard to sort and discard. Dump your backpacks, gals, clean up time. Some stuff we thought important may be a heavy burden now!

Prayer: Lord, create in me a new heart and renew a right spirit within me. Examine me, Lord, and reveal any wicked way in me. Cleanse me through the power of the Holy Spirit and fill me up with You. You alone are my rescue from my selfish ways. I am ready to put off my selfish nature and put on Godliness.

Hide in My Heart: "With regard to your former way of life, *put off* your old self which is to be made new in the attitude of your minds; and *put on* the new self, created to be like God in true righteousness and holiness." (Ephesians 4:22-24)

Choose Today: I choose to put off the old ungodly behaviors and to put-on my new self.

Week 34, Day 2. Read: Romans 8:5–10.
Journal: If you are human, you act according to human nature. Does this discourage you? Do you feel *never good enough* to please God? Remember, *your salvation is secure in Christ.* You are not trying to earn your way to Godliness. *In Christ you are already a new creation.* Our efforts align us with God to renew our minds and become a victorious. Journal what this means to you.
Action Tool: Circle the "Put-Offs" in the lesson that are weaknesses for you.

Week 34, Day 3. Read: Colossians 3:1–14.
Journal: Note in the reading, "get rid", "take off" and, "clothe yourself". Ask the Lord to show you the "put-ons" that are the antidote to your target "put-offs" from the lesson. It may not be the exact opposite word, but a quality needed for growth.

Action Tool:

1. In His strength, I put off_____; I put on_____.
2. When tempted: U-TURN.
3. Repent from acting out the "Put-Off". Then act according to your "Put-On".

Week 34, Day 4. Read: Colossians 3:12–14.
Journal: Putting on love must be the underlying motive for all we do. Where are you falling short? Where are you growing?
Action Tool: Practice Put-Off and Put-On.

Week 34 Day 5. Read: Colossians 3:15–17.
Journal: Give thanks for any success in putting-off and putting-on. Pray your words and deeds will exemplify Jesus.
Action Tool: Sing, Dance, Turn up the Music! Celebrate Jesus!

Mocha Machines and Other Weighty Stuff
Week 35, Day 1

Submit yourself, then to God. Resist the devil, and he will flee from you. Come near to God and he will come near to you.

(James 4:7–8)

> Oh, my goodness, I packed my battery-operated mocha machine all this way. What was I thinking? I was the one who said, "Only the necessities". Off it goes on the mules. And this rock collection stowed in the bottom of my pack, discarded! Whoa, Monica, you brought your tablet and cell phone? Reception is nonexistent out here. Stacy, what is that two-inch thick book? A list of everyone who has ever hurt you? That is a definite put off. How about burning it?

Great list of put-offs and put-ons in last week's lesson. Nice intentions. Almost impossible to live out. Yes, without God, impossible to put off sin and put on Godliness. Even with God, the new nature requires a moment by moment choice. Yet, he has not left us powerless. He says we can do it, therefore, we can.

> His divine power has given us everything we need for life and godliness through our knowledge of him who called us by his own glory and goodness. Through these he has given us his very great and precious promises so that through them you may participate in the divine nature and escape the corruption in the world (and yourself)

caused by evil desires (self-centered motivations and ungodly character traits in you and in others who affect you). For this reason, make every effort to add to your faith, goodness, and to goodness, knowledge, and to knowledge, self-control, and to self-control, perseverance, and to perseverance, godliness, and to godliness, brotherly kindness, and to brotherly kindness, love. For, if you possess these qualities in increasing measure, they will keep you from being ineffective and unproductive in your knowledge of our Lord Jesus Christ.

(2 Peter 1:3–8)

Our emotions triggered by the actions of other will assault us. If you are alive, this is guaranteed. We cannot avoid it unless we harden our heart to the point of not caring. Still, God has not left us alone in this struggle.

> For God, who said, 'Let light shine out of darkness', made his light shine in our hearts to give us the light of knowledge of the glory of God in the face of Christ. But we have this treasure in jars of clay to show that this all-surpassing power is from God and not from us. We are hard pressed on every side, but not crushed; perplexed, but not in despair, persecuted, but not abandoned; struck down, but not destroyed. We always carry around in our body the death of Jesus so that the life of Jesus may also be revealed in our body. For we who are alive are always being given over to death for Jesus' sake, so that his life may be revealed in our mortal body. So then, death is at work in us, but life is at work in you.

(2 Corinthians 4:6–11)

Mountain of Gloom Weather forecast: Hard pressed (stressed), crushed (depressed), perplexed (anxious), persecuted (hurt by someone), struck down (belittled), death (abandonment, loss, destruction, and evil). Attire for this weather: Truth, righteousness, the gospel, faith, salvation, scripture, the Holy Spirit, prayer, being alert.

> Finally, be strong in the Lord and in his mighty power. Put on the full armor of God so that you can take your stand against the devil's schemes. For our struggle is not against flesh and blood, but against the rulers, against the authorities, against the powers of this dark world and against the spiritual forces of evil in the heavenly realms. There, *put on* the full armor of God, so that when the day of evil comes, you may be able to stand your ground, and after you have done everything, to stand. Stand firm then, with the belt of truth buckled around your waist, with the breastplate of righteousness in place, and with your feet fitted with the readiness that comes from the gospel of peace. In addition to all this, take up the shield of faith, with which you can extinguish all the flaming arrows of the evil one. Take the helmet of salvation and the sword of the Spirit which is the word of God. And pray in the Spirit on all occasions with all kinds of prayers and requests. With this in mind, be alert and always keep on praying for all the saints.
>
> (Ephesians 6:10–18)

Put offs, put-ons, forecast, attire. Good instruction, yet the bottom line is, "How do I put it into action in my life?" So, you have identified a characteristic you must put-off. You want to put-on (clothe yourself) in a Godly characteristic.

Make time to prepare a battle plan. For an example, I highlighted "self-pity" on the put-off list. "Thanksgiving, praise and contentment" impressed me as the antidote to "self-pity". In prayer, God gave me a plan to cope the instant self-pity spirals me down to despair. The plan affirmed both night and morning align my heart with Godliness.

My Put-On Battle Plan against Self-Pity:

- ❖ <u>Agree</u> with God that self-pity is destructive.
- ❖ In His strength, I <u>put off</u> "Self-Pity"; I <u>put on</u> "Thanksgiving and Praise."

- ❖ Say to myself, no <u>self-pity, no excuses</u>!
- ❖ <u>List 10</u> items "worthy of praise".
- ❖ <u>Affirm:</u> "Being sorry for my self is destructive. It expresses dissatisfaction in God's provision. Self-pity shows my lack of trust in God and destroys my contentment. The grace and power of God enables victory over this sin. I choose victory."

Before battle against the devil and your selfish nature, fortify with prayer. Gird yourself with battle gear and a plan of attack. Tackling one Put-Off at a time with perseverance, God will lead you to victory.

> Therefore, we do not lose heart. Though outwardly we are wasting away (getting old, illness, hardships), yet inwardly, we are being renewed day by day.
>
> (2 Corinthians 4:16)

He changes our hearts to become more kind, loving, wise, at peace, and joyful, so we can navigate the crush of life without despair. God says it. So be it.

> I am energized after a real bacon and egg breakfast, thanks to the mule handlers. Hate to see them go. Wish they could carry me on out. My feet hurt; my back hurts; it is just too hard. I am so tired… Whoa, Anne, don't go there. U-turn! Thanks for this wonderful opportunity, Lord, to share this journey with my sisters. Thank you for using the sufferings of my early journeys to encourage my fellow pilgrims. Praise your name for working this together for good. So be it.

Prayer: Mighty God, Creator of the Universe, come with me into war against my strongholds. Reveal your battle plan for me. Amen.

Hide in My Heart: "For though we live in the world, we do not wage war as the world does. The weapons we fight with are not the weapons of the world. On the contrary, they have divine power to demolish strongholds. We demolish arguments and every pretension that sets itself up against the

knowledge of God, and we take captive every thought to make it obedient to Christ" (2 Corinthians 10: 4–5).
Choose Today: By your power, I will bring my thoughts captive to Jesus!

Week 35, Day 2. Read: Ephesians 6:10–18.
Journal: What "put-off" God has placed on your heart as needing immediate attention. Create, together with God, your own "Battle Plan" to put-off unrighteousness and put-on righteousness. Take your time; bathe the process in prayer.
Action Tool: Work on your Battle Plan

Week 35, Day 3. Read: 2 Corinthians 10:3–6.
Journal: Rereading the scripture. How does God's word give you hope? What are our weapons? What do we need for victory?
Action Tool: Work on your Battle Plan.

Week 35, Day 4. Read: 2 Peter 1:3-8
Journal: Even though our salvation with Christ is secure, what renders us ineffective? What action is needed when we fail and get discouraged?
Action Tool: Sit still, imagining an incident requiring your Battle Plan, then think through applying the plan.

Week 35, Day 5. Read: 2 Corinthians 4:5–12 and 2 Corinthians 4:16.
Journal: Where are you feeling crushed in your life? How are you tempted to lose heart? Claim victory today. Apply your battle plan, saying, "You and Me, God."
Action Tool: Apply your Battle Plan.

Resting in the Garden of God
Week 36, Day 1

> **Now the Lord God had planted a garden in the east, in Eden; and there he put the man he had formed. And the Lord God made all kinds of trees grow out of the ground—trees that were pleasing to the eye and good for food.**
>
> **(Genesis 2:8–9)**

> Well gals, our packs clean, our food supplies renewed, a good breakfast in our bellies, Serenity Lake at our feet. Shall we rest and worship today in the garden of God?

> And God blessed the seventh day and made it holy because on it he rested from all the work of creating that he had done.
>
> (Genesis 2:3)

In His garden paradise, God brought the woman to the man. He provided abundant food and lush vegetation, then rested. Resting was God's idea. It restores and heals mankind. Following his example take time apart to mend your body from work and your mind from stress. A drink of cool water and a heart filled with worship as we relax in the garden brings healing to the bones. Being out in nature, in a quiet little corner of our yard, or out in the stunning pristine wilderness, in a city park or you-pick-strawberry-plot reconnects us to our Lord.

> For since the creation of the world God's invisible qualities—his eternal power and divine nature—have been clearly seen, being understood from what has been made so that men/women are without excuse.
>
> (Romans 1:20)

If we have eyes to see, resting in the garden gets our focus off ourselves and onto the creator. It distracts us from our crazy, stressful lives and fills us up, if only for a moment, with beauty. The pensive mind generates creativity. Science confirms quiet pondering and beauty create endorphins that lift our spirits. It lowers our blood pressure and raises our serotonin levels. His creation draws us closer to God. So, as part of the healing or staying-whole process, retreat often into nature.

Long ago, linked with nature due to necessity, rest happened with the ebb and flow of daylight, but no longer. Our busy electronic age consumes us indoors. Media claims our eyes and ears. Carve out time to detach from gadgets and screens, yes, even cell phones. Stroll in the garden. Learn to be comfortable with quiet, with the song of birds and chatter of squirrels. Concentrate on thanksgiving and praise. True rest and worship results from a quiet soul.

Some days, the heavens bless God's garden with rain. Once backpacking in the desert, the ground was expectedly dry and barren. Overnight a squall burst upon us. The next morning, packing up drenched sleeping bags, we found the desert carpeted with tiny purple and yellow flowers. God's gift of water brought forth life and vegetation. Water is a miracle. It is the only liquid that is clean and cleanses, gives life to creatures and recycles itself. Without it we die. With it we thrive. If there were no rain, no winter storms, our earth would be a desert. We need the ebb and flow of seasons in our life. Times of sorrow and stress followed by times of quiet and restoration.

If we are willing, God cultivates a sanctuary with in us, a refreshing place of shade, light, water, and spiritual fruit. His plan requires dwelling in this garden, abiding in Jesus.

> As my Father has loved me, so have I loved you. Now remain (abide) in my love.
>
> (John 15:9)

He meets us and creates the rest within our heart, mind and soul.

- ○ The Lord is my shepherd; I shall not be in want. He makes me lie down in green pastures; he leads me beside quiet waters; he restores my soul. (Psalm 23: 1–3)

- My soul finds rest in God alone; my salvation comes from him. (Psalm 62:1)
- Come to me, all you who are weary and burdened, and I will give you rest. Take my yoke upon you and learn from me, for I am gentle and humble in heart, and you will find rest for your souls. For my yoke is easy and my burden is light. (Matthew 11:28–30)

Where is your restorative secret garden? A place away from the pressures of life? What scenic vista or leafy nook speaks beauty and calm to your heart? Come, let's go there and worship the Lord.

"In the Garden"

I come to the garden alone while the dew is still on the roses
And the voice I hear falling on my ear the son of God discloses
And he walks with me and he talks with me and he tells me I am his own
And the joy we share as we tarry there none other has ever known.
Charles A. Miles, 1913

"Joyful, joyful, I adore thee, God of wonders, God of grace." As I focus on praise, my heart fills with joy despite the sorrows of my life. I could not, would not, want to live without the joy of the Lord. Oh, come, look! A mama duck and a bevy of fluffy baby ducklings by the side of the lake!

Prayer: Dear Jesus, may I walk with you in the Garden of God? Teach me to absorb your beauty, to see your presence in the glories of nature. Thank you, O my God, for creating all this for me. Amen

Hide in My Heart: "I am the true vine and my Father is the gardener... Abide (remain) in me and I will remain in you. No branch can bear fruit by itself; it must remain in the vine. Neither can you bear fruit unless you remain in me" (John 15:1–5).

Choose Today: I choose today to rest in my Jesus and walk with him in a quiet place.

Week 36, Day 2. Read: Psalm 100
Journal: Sit quietly, contemplating Psalm 100. Then journal your praise and worship.
Action Tool: Go online, listen and sing along to "In the Garden". https://www.youtube.com/watch?v=9aIhta9exts

Week 36, Day 3. Read: Psalm 65:13, Genesis 2:15
Journal: Describe a lovely garden or scene that brings joy. Sketch a picture of this place in your journal and draw yourself in the midst.
Action Tool: Visit God's garden often. Walk in a park. Lift your eyes to the mountains or sky. Absorb the scenery. When indoors take your mind to a vista of natural grandeur.

Week 36, Day 4. Read: John 17:13–26 and Psalm 46:10.
Journal: What plagues your thoughts at night preventing deep sleep? Journal and pray about your resting issues.
Action Tool: Create a sleep ritual for the evening. Suggestions: Turn off the TV one hour before bedtime. Lower the lights. Play soft music or a white noise machine. Read Psalm 23 or 100.

Week 36, Day 5. Read: John 15:1–10 and Matthew 11:28–30
Journal: Abide–Await; endure without yielding; to remain stable or fixed in a state; to accept without objection; to continue, stay, bear; endure. * Contemplate on today's scriptures and the meaning of abide. Journal how the Lord speaks to your heart on abiding and resting in Him. *Webster's New Collegiate Dictionary.
Action Tool: Create your garden nook in your house and/or in your yard to rest a moment by still waters. Suggestions: House plants, a view out the window, a terrarium, a picture on the wall, a tabletop fountain, or a bench in the yard. Each time you enter these green pastures "abide" in Jesus.

Gurgling Brook
Week 37, Day 1

> **Sons and daughters are a heritage from the Lord, children a reward from him. Blessed is the woman whose quiver is full of them.**
>
> **(Psalm 127: 3a, 5a)**

All these days hiking and nary a child on the trail. Look yonder, ladies, a family camped by the gurgling brook. Laundry lines, food bins, kid clutter. Their camp appears well entrenched here on the Mountain of Gloom. One, two, three… eight children. Whew! That's a handful.

With eager anticipation we await the birth of our first child. We delight in their coos, gurgles and giggles, then wallow in fatigue or postpartum depression. We beam with pride when they first ride a bike or make a wise decision as a youth, yet they frustrate us by whining, ignoring instructions and rebellious attitudes. Even our adult children, though a source of great joy as they become confident and productive, may also cause significant pain when poor choices bring serious and long-lasting consequences. Along the way, every family ends up camping for a spell on the Mountain of Gloom.

Remember, God is our parent and we are disobedient, stubborn, rebellious, unfaithful, and selfish. It takes a lifetime of yielding to His teaching to exemplify the fruit of the spirit… kindness, goodness, gentleness, patience and self-control. Why would we expect our children to be any different? And yet, our impatience and exasperation are abundantly clear when our children do not "hop to it" with one sharp word from us. Our actions mold and shape whom our children become. The child has a choice to yield and grow into an honorable adult or not. But as for us as parents, it is our job to lay the best foundation possible. As with everything else, we will fall short, yet press on we must.

> Let the little children come to me, and do not hinder them, for the kingdom of heaven belongs to such as these.
> (Matthew 19:14)

God grants us grace and forgiveness, blessings and consequence, boundaries and freedom, love and discipline. Good parenting models these qualities to our children. Create a living picture of Jesus for your little ones, teens and grown children through your actions. Yes, I know, how?

Visualize yourself as a little girl, naughty, frightened and lost. Your loving father finds you. Gathering you into his arms, he whispers, "Here I am". He sings as he walks home quieting your anxiety with his love. Once inside, your father sits you on his knee, gazes in your eyes asking, "What happened?"

"I got lost."

"Why did you get lost?"

"I ran away when you called me."

"How did lost feel?"

"Scary."

"I understand. The natural consequence to running away is to get lost and scared. It is OK to feel scared; it is not OK to run away when Daddy told you to follow him. Daddy loves you. He wants you to make good choices. Take three minutes in the big chair, then come talk to Daddy."

"Calm now? What do you need to say?"

"I'm sorry for running away."

"I forgive you," Daddy whispers as he cuddles his little one.

> The LORD your God is with you, he is mighty to save.
> He will take great delight in you, he will quiet you with his love, he will rejoice over you with singing.
> (Zephaniah 3:17 NKJV)

What an incredible word picture of God's rescue when we lose control. Despite their rebelliousness, our children require patience and kindness as we guide them towards good choices. Affirm your love during correction and discipline.

Baby 101. Nurtured, nourished, held close, safe in loving arms, baby thrives. My daughters experienced little comfort until adopted into our home at three and four years old. The orphanage in Romania functioned with three adults caring for 125 toddlers and babies. Deprivation of touch and love injured brain growth. Cognitive development was seriously impaired. Having never received loved, nor experienced positive results from their actions, my girls had no sense of right or wrong, no internal boundaries to control their behaviors. They would not make eye contact, exhibited no ability to bond with humans and showed no remorse. It took many years of prayer, dedication, trial and error, and love to overcome damage done during their early years. So, moms and dads, do everything you can to give your baby security. Quiet them with your love! Rejoice over them with singing. For many couples, day care is an economic necessity. Seek a patient, gentle environment which models Godly love and consequences. At home, soak your infant in touch, talk and giggles. They will absorb your love.

Behavior of all mankind results in consequences. Humans have two choices: to obey (the laws of love, society, kindness) therefore receive a blessing (reward, paycheck, respect). Or disobey (disregard the laws of love, society, kindness) thus reap negative consequences (loss of job, divorce, pain).

> This day I call the heavens and the earth as witnesses against you that I have set before you, life and death, blessings and curses (consequences). Now choose life, so that you and your children may live.
>
> (Deuteronomy 30:19)

Children who understand parents are not requesting blind obedience but good choices, more often choose well as children or adults.

> Teach (the statues of God) to your children, talking about them as you walk along the road, when you lie down and when you get up.
>
> (Deuteronomy 11:19)

> Fathers and mothers do not exasperate your children; instead, bring them up in the training and instruction of the Lord.
>
> (Ephesians 6:4)

> Let us not love with words or speech but with actions and in truth.
>
> (1 John 3:18

Good instruction. Sound easy? Not so, because of our own impatient reactions. I get it! I lived it! I could be more patient with twenty-two second graders than with two little girls. Monica remembers my tantrum while teaching her fractions. One day she responded flippant and uncooperative. Frustrated, I threw the papers on the floor, jumped up and down, and ran around in circles. Monica laughed hysterically. My behavior just encouraged her bad behavior. Let's make Mama do this again! This is fun!

Room time for Monica. Time out for me in conference with the Almighty. His lesson: Bring my frustrations before Him. Calm down. Take five. Then filter proposed actions through the word of God. My actions must:

Test #1. Not provoke. (Ephesians 6:4)
Test #2. Promote love. (1 Corinthians 13:4)
Test #3. Be wise. (James 3:17)
Test #4. Be of one mind with my husband. (Ephesians 5:21)
Test #6. Only speak words and actions that benefit. (Ephesians 4:29)

After parental time out, speak the truth in love. "Let's talk, sweetie. Mommy lost it. Will you forgive me? We both struggle with fractions. Let's create a plan with rewards and consequences. How about we cut up candy bars for fractions? A good attitude you get to eat them. Bad attitude they go in the disposal. What do you think?"

Of course, this concept must be modified by age. For the wee one, very little explanation. For example, "Choice one is to obey Mommy and get a hug; choice two is to be naughty and get a timeout." Another example, "It is OK to feel _____. It is not OK to do _____. Time-out chair for 3 minutes. I'm setting the timer."

For the teen, a written statement of blessings and consequences posted on the refrigerator is often more successful than verbal discussions. Teens respond best when they participate in creating the chart. For example:

> Situation 1: Speak respectfully to mom with your words and tone of voice.
>
> Blessing: Mom will listen and carefully consider your request.
>
> Consequence: Disrespectful words and tone of voice end the conversation before it starts. An automatic "No" will result.
>
> Situation 2: Going out and coming home. Discuss times and events with a parent. Arrive home at the time planned or call with a reason and/or permission for the delay.
>
> Blessing: More freedom to make your own choices at coming and going.
>
> Consequences: Arriving home late, not calling, going elsewhere than planned will result in less freedom, more restrictions and ultimately grounding.

For adult children who are making bad choices, remind your child of blessings and consequences, then step back and pray for him/her. Do not rescue them from natural consequences. God gives us the freedom and doles out good or difficult consequences according to our choices. Let him do so with your adult children. It is time to "let go and let God".

> Hello Folks, what a great camp set up. Have you camped on the Mountain of Gloom long? Three years! Oh, my goodness. But you are packing up and moving on tomorrow? That is fantastic. Have all eight children learned to obey? No? Oh, you, the parents, have learned to walk peacefully with your God and speak the truth in love to your children? Wow! Sure, we would love to join you round the campfire for S'mores.

Prayer: Lord, in the moments of parenting, we are often clueless what to do. Parenting overwhelms us. We frequently react without thinking followed by depression about our children and parenting. We lay prostrate before you in our need. Here I am, Lord, show me how to parent.
Hide in My Heart: "Fathers and mothers, do not exasperate your children; instead, bring them up in the training and instruction of the Lord." (Ephesians 6:4).
Choose Today: I choose to trust God with my children, leaning on Him to show me how to parent.

Week 37, Day 2. Read: Proverbs 20:11, Ephesians 6:1, Deuteronomy 30:19–20a.
Journal: When you get a new puppy, does it automatically sit, stay, come, potty outside? Of course not. It takes months of consistent training. Trainers start with tiny behavior changes for the dog with plenty of rewards. Yet we often expect a haphazard approach is sufficient for our children. We parent as we were parented, for better or worse. What changes are needed to reflect the character of God in your home?
Action Tool: Quiet with Love Parenting. Work on loving contact:

- Greet with a smile, a touch, a word of encouragement when you pass the child.
- Make eye contact when communicating.
- Listen to the child with full attention. "Tell me the story."
- Affirm, "It is Ok to _____. It is not Ok to _____."
- Use the Calming Time Out Chair for everyone in the family including parents.
- Remain calm yet do not give in to a disrespectful or disobedient child.
- Parent apologizes when the parent fails.
- Forgiveness is modeled and taught.
- God's word is the standard for living.

Week 37, Day 3. Read: Proverbs 22:6
Journal: Proverbs 22:6 is often viewed as a promise. However, there is no guarantee our children will follow God or return to Him. God gave

everyone a choice to follow him or not, to choose life or choose death, our children also. Even so, statistics reveal many adults reared in church return to faith. Therefore, Godly parenting is crucial. List three behaviors your child needs to learn, improve or change.

Action Tool: Quiet with Love Expectations and Time Out

Teach and model expected behaviors and self-control. Explain blessings come from obedience and good choices. Consequences result from disobedience and poor choices. Plan purposeful training sessions:

Clear Expectations

1. Identify behavior child needs to learn, improve, change.
2. Write expected age-appropriate action.
3. Parent demonstrates the behavior for the child. Parent gets the reward.
4. Repeat action together with child. Make it fun. Child gets the reward.
5. Practice daily until this behavior becomes a habit.

Week 37, Day 4. Read: 1 Timothy 3:4, Ephesians 4:2, 4:29 and 6:4.

Journal: How do you as a parent exasperate, put-down, provoke, and be disrespectful to your children. These actions by parents can create sad, frightened or rebellious children. God calls us to respond to our children with gentleness and long suffering. "Gentleness" means not dealing rudely or with harshness. "Long suffering" describes restraint in the face of opposition. It is calmness and patience under provocation. Today, list your words or actions which are harmful to your children.

Action Tool: Quiet with Love Discussion Time.

Discussion Time

1. Tell me the story of what happened?
2. What harm was caused?
3. How can the harm be repaired?
4. It is Ok to _____, it is not OK to _____? (Child fills in the blanks if possible.)
5. What do you need to say? (apology, etc.)

6. I am proud of you for working this through.

Week 37, Day 5. Read: Psalm 127:3, 1 Timothy 5:10.
Journal: Our children are a blessing and inheritance from God. Do we treat them as such or as an annoyance? Do we delight in them? Concentrate today on imparting joy to your children. Make a list of how you delight in your children. Write honest praises for each child. Plan for good times with the kids this week.
Action Tool: Quiet with Love Walk Along the Road

- Pray and memorize scripture together every day.
- Family –Gather at a meal and read from a child appropriate devotional.
- Praise Hunt–Walk the yard and the house with kids discovering thankworthy things.
- God sightings–Dinner or car conversation. How have you seen God in action today?
- May I have a hug–Ask for this instead of whining

Baby's Breath
Week 38, Day 1

> For you created my inmost being; you knit me together in my mother's womb. I praise you because I am fearfully and wonderfully made; your works are wonderful; I know that full well.
>
> (Psalm 139: 13–14)

> Monica, sweetie, the young pilgrim, Kara, over there is in turmoil over a huge decision she must make very soon. Would you walk with her a bit and share your story?

"Hi Kara, my Mom says you are having a struggle that maybe I could relate to. What's up?"

"Oh Monica, I'm pregnant and don't have any idea what I am going to do. The guy wants nothing to do with me. I haven't told my parents yet and I just am so messed up without a job or anything."

"Boy, I get it. The same thing happened to me when I was about your age. I met a guy that I thought was cute, ended up sleeping with him and got pregnant. I didn't know what to do."

"Were you scared?"

"I was really scared, Kara. I was like, "This can't happen!" I thought, "If I ignore this craziness it will all go away." I knew I wasn't ready to be a mom."

"Did you want to get an abortion?"

"I did at very first. But then I realized that wasn't an option for me. This was a human baby, my baby. It was already a beautiful baby even if it was only the size of a stamp. No way could I kill this little baby."

"Oh, Monica, I don't want an abortion either. But maybe I will have to do it. This is just so hard. I don't know what to do. What did you do?"

"I knew that I couldn't take care of a baby. I was just a kid myself. I had no job, no car, I was living with my parents at the time and afraid of their reaction. There was no way I could do this. I also knew about adoption, cuz I was adopted. I knew that some couples have tried for so long to have kids and couldn't. I thought, "Maybe one of them would be ok for my baby." This was a very hard decision, but once I got pregnant, everything I did had to be for my little peanut."

"Wasn't it hard? Harder even than abortion?"

"Oh, my goodness, Kara, was it hard. I think abortion might have been easier, but I kept thinking, it's like I would have been just flushing my baby down the toilet. I knew I would regret it every day of my life afterwards. This kid was going to be a mini me. I wanted to know how this little peanut was going to grow up. I wasn't going to be able to be there for her first steps, first day of school, her first words and so much more. Adoption is hard, but again, it's a decision I made for my daughter. She means the world to me. I am so grateful I have her in my life. My adoption is open. I get to know so much about her and her life. I got the best of both worlds."

"Did you want to change your mind?"

"Yes, when she was born, I fell in love with her. I knew that I still wasn't ready to be a mom, just cuz she looked perfect. Besides, the family I had chosen was so excited to have a daughter, that it would have devastated them."

"Why didn't you just keep the baby and raise her yourself?"

"Believe me, I wanted to. She was perfect. Eight pounds, four ounces and 22.5 inches long. She was gorgeous. But I had to think about how I would raise this little one. I had no housing of my own, no financial resources, no car. I was a hot mess myself. I was not about to put her in a homeless shelter with me. That's not right. I needed to focus on getting my life put back together and having a baby would have made things really hard. I knew that the family I picked out was going to be perfect for my precious daughter. She needed to have stability, something I sure didn't have at the time. Again, once I had her, it wasn't about me anymore. It was about her and what she needed. I wanted her to have a mom and a dad who would provide a loving home."

"What if I want to keep my baby? Do you think that would be wrong?"

"Keeping your baby wouldn't be wrong. You need to look at the big picture. Are you ready to be a mom to a little human being who depends solely on you? Babies are cute but at 2:00am when they are screaming and crying, it gets hard. Are you ready to not get sleep for months at a time? I know for me, I love my sleep. You must remember that once you have a child, it not about you anymore. I know this sounds harsh but believe me, it's true. Everything you do will be for that child. Do you have a boyfriend that will be willing to help you? I know with my partner, he up and left. I was stuck. Just remember, Kara, I am not telling you that you must do adoption. I am trying to talk to you from experience. Depending on your circumstances, maybe it will work for you to keep your baby. I wish I could have, but at the time, I just couldn't."

"You seem so normal, Monica, even happy. I don't think I will ever feel that way again."

"Normal? Well it has taken a lot of therapy and God in my life to help me get to where I am at now. I have had a really hard time lately, but I know that I have a good support system in place, counselors, family and friends to help me. Oh, and if you have post-partum depression, don't be afraid to get more help. I was and am still on medications that help with my depression. It gets hard no matter what decision you make."

"What about now, Monica, do you ever get to see your daughter?"

"Yes!!!!!! I have an open adoption. I get to see her four times a year. I get pictures, phone calls and letters and drawings my daughter makes for me. Yes, she knows I am her birth mother. She is happy to know me. She tells her friends at school that she has two mommies who love her and that she is special. I remember a visit a while back. She was sitting on my lap and said, "I know where I came from." I asked her where. She said, "From your tummy," pointing to my tummy. It was so cute. She asked, "Did I move a lot?" "Yes," I said, "a ton." "How did you sleep if I was kicking you?" I said, "I didn't sleep much cuz you were a very squirmy baby." She then said, "So you slept when I was asleep in your tummy." Yes, indeed. She is a smart cookie.

She is now six years old and is full of life and love. She has a great home. Her adoptive parents are doing an amazing job with her. They love her beyond words can even begin to express. I know that I chose the best family for her. I am forever grateful to God, my family, the adoption agency and my daughter's adoptive parents for how she has turned out. She looks just like me, except blonde hair and blue eyes. Honestly, if I chose abortion or chose tried to raise her myself, I don't think I would be doing as well as I am today. Oh, my goodness, if she didn't even exist, I would be missing out on so much fun and love. I also know that she wouldn't be happy and doing as well as she is with her adoptive family if she was I with me. This is not to say I don't love my daughter or want her. Believe me, I never knew how much I could love until I had her. And of course, I want her, but I know that God had other plans for her and me both.

"Yea, so where is God in all this? I feel as if He just doesn't care about me. I feel so lost and rejected and lonely and just want to be done with it all."

"I feel that way so often, Kara, but I was the one who got myself pregnant. I can't blame that on God. He cares. He put you and I on this trip together, didn't he? What are the chances of that, someone who understands what you are going through? Just hang on. Why don't you call me up when you get down and we can talk until you figure everything out? Here's a verse to cling to, Jeremiah 29:11. This has been my favorite verse. A go-to verse for me when I feel like things are all wrong and out of control.

> For I know the plans I have for you declares the Lord,
> plans to prosper you and not to harm you, plans to give
> you a future and a hope.
>
> Jeremiah 29:11

This verse helps me see that God is in control. Even though we may not see it in the moment, I can look back on my life and with my adoption process. God planned everything according to His glory. I see how blessed I am and how my daughter is from the decisions I have made. Another verse is, "Never will I leave you or forsake you." I think that's Hebrews 13:5.

> Baby's Breath is tucked in with every rose bought by a sweetheart on Valentine's Day. Little white sprinkles of flowers together with a red rose, love symbolized, even for our babies. Thank you, Monica for sharing with Kara.

Prayer: My Jesus, we praise you that through our suffering we can comfort our others. Help us love and care for our sisters who are struggling with this issue of bearing a surprise child.

Hide in My Heart: "If anyone of you lacks wisdom, he should ask God, who gives generously to all without finding fault, and it will be given to him."

Choose Today: I am open to your teaching me, Lord, even with hard decisions. I will follow you.

Week 38, Day 2. Read: Psalm 139.

Journal: Ask God to speak to you through His written word. Underline phrases which call out to you in today's scripture. Copy them in your journal.

Action Tool: Allow God to search your heart and reveal His wisdom to you.

Week 38, Day 3. Read: James 3:17–18.

Journal: What difficult decision are you being called to make that perhaps goes against the ways of the world? How does the wisdom of heaven apply to that situation?

Action Tool: Focus on a difficult decision. Answer each question, then filter your answers with the instruction from James 3:17-18

- ❖ Am I willing to wait upon the Lord for a decision that brings righteousness and peace?
- ❖ If I am married, have my husband and I come to one mind regarding this decision?
- ❖ Have I regarded what the word of God has to say on this matter?
- ❖ Have I sought Godly counsel and considered their wisdom?
- ❖ Does this decision bring wholeness and benefit to those affected by it?
- ❖ Does this decision bring me a deep sense of quiet and peace?

Week 38, Day 4. Read: Jeremiah 29:11.

Journal: Pray for God to bring to you someone who needs comfort from your life experiences. Seek wisdom to comfort them not through human reasoning but through Godly encouragement. Write what God is placing on your heart.

Action Tool: Write a letter of comfort. Share the scriptures. This is not a time to lecture, scold or instruct them. Simply love on this suffering or confused one.

Week 38, Day 5. Read: Psalm 139: 13–16 and Jeremiah 1:4–5.
Journal: What do these scriptures speak to your heart about the unborn? Apply the scriptural questions and wisdom from Day 2 and Day 3 to any decision regarding an unborn child. Sit quietly in prayer and contemplation, then journal as God leads you.
Action Tool: How might you bless a girl you know who had an abortion, given a child up for adoption, or is a young unprepared single parent? Be sensitive as these are painful issues. Pray for a creative way to bless the person God brings to your mind.

Sweet Romance Falls
Week 39, Day 1

> **Then the Lord God made a woman from the rib he had taken out of the man and he brought her to the man. The man said, "This is now bone of my bones and flesh of my flesh."**
>
> **Genesis 2: 22-23**

> Thundering water falling into a deep pool, misty fringes kissing us with sprinkles, boulders upon which to sit and gaze, Sweet Romance Falls illustrates love. Falling in love consumes one with a frothing foam of emotions, wonderful and painful. True love endures a thunderous process of wearing away the jagged edges through the seasons. As you ladies know, faithful, lifelong love is not easy. Today, as we climb, let us explore God's view on love between a husband and wife.

A young couple walking on a white sandy beach, an old couple sitting on a bench holding hands, a man and a woman embracing, sealing their love with an impassioned kiss… this is the most popular theme of movies and of life itself. The story of love. Naturally, the world being fallen, the movie industry has morphed the story of love into the story of sex.

Regardless of today's casual attitude about sex, ultimately most women desire love with a man who will cherish and uplift them. What if your marriage did not start out with "being-in-love" or you no longer "feel" in love? It matters not; love is from God, is a gift of God. He can bring love where no love exists through our obedience to him.

True love, forever after love, more in love today than yesterday, may begin with a burst of euphoria, yet, real love is not an emotion; it is action. True love requires a commitment to act loving. Falling in love produces good-feeling hormones which fade as real life takes over. Choosing to act loving despite the circumstances creates a deep abiding love that grows stronger and more beautiful over a lifetime.

> Dear children let us not love with words or tongue but with actions and in truth.
> (1 John 3:18)

> My command is this: Love each other as I have loved you. Greater love has no one than this that he lay down his life for his friends (husband, children).
> (John 15:12)

With my selfish nature, how in the world do I love with selflessness? Especially, when the world proclaims self-gratification and self-esteem. Obedience to the word of God is the answer. We become convicted by embedding his words deep into our subconscious, by pondering and memorizing them. Then by acting upon what we have learned, through the power of God, we become love in action. As we grow in Godly behavior our self-respect and self-esteem flowers. We transform into a caring, peace-giving woman.

> Love is patient, love is kind, it does not envy, it does not boast, it is not proud. It is not rude, it is not self-seeking, it is not easily angered, it keeps no record of wrongs. Love does not delight in evil but rejoices with the truth. It always protects, always trusts, always hopes, always perseveres. Love never fails.
> (1 Corinthians 13:4–8a)

Impossible, you say. Yes, without the Lord, it is impossible. We are fallen, so perfection is beyond our ability. Jesus is the personification of love. Only He can love perfectly. But you, dear one, walking with the Lord, day-by-day will be strengthened and renewed. He promises.

> I can do all things, through Christ who strengths me.
> (Philippians 4:13)

Do not for a moment think I have it easy, ladies, while you do not. The ups and downs today are still tempestuous. There are disappointments and dramas, devastating events and major depressions, cross words and angry flare-ups generated by family members and out of my control. Waking in the middle of the night worried and depressed is common for me even today. Every day requires remembering to seek the face of God. To choose love in action when I prefer to withdraw is extremely hard and often painful. If I can, with the strength of God, you can too.

> Therefore, I urge you, brothers and sisters, in view of God's mercy, to offer your bodies as a living sacrifice, holy and pleasing to God—this is your true and proper worship. Do not conform to the pattern of this world but be transformed by the renewing of your mind. Then you will be able to test and approve what God's will is—his good, pleasing and perfect will.
>
> (Romans 12:1–2)

So, let's get to it; one day, one moment, one choice at a time.

> I know, hurting sisters, sometimes love seems to fail when you pour your life out for someone and he remains hurtful or leaves or a child goes wayward. Remember, we are not responsible for the choices of anyone but ourselves. Therefore, enrich your life by choosing to love through action. It is worth the hike.

Prayer: Lord, teach me to love in action. Enable me to personify real love, Father, the kind in 1 Corinthians 13. I am willing; In the name and through the power of my Jesus.

Hide in My Heart: "Love is patient, love is kind, it does not envy, it does not boast, it is not proud. It is not rude, it is not self-seeking, it is not easily angered, it keeps no record of wrongs. Love does not delight in evil

but rejoices with the truth. It always protects, always trusts, always hopes, always perseveres. Love never fails" (1 Corinthians 13:4–8).
Choose Today: My heart desire is to become known for my ability to love despite my shortcomings and the actions of others.

Week 39, Day 2. Reread: 1 Corinthians 13:4–8.
Journal: Ask the Lord to reveal your short comings regarding loving actions. List them. Isolate one shortcoming. Confess and lay this habit at His feet agreeing with Him you need to change.
Action Tool: Draw a heart over the qualities in 1 Corinthian 13: 3-4 in which you are growing each day. Draw a circle around the qualities needing serious transformation in you through the work of Jesus.

Week 39, Day 3. Read: John 15:12 and 1 John 3:18.
Journal: "Your friend" in today's scripture includes your husband and children. Write out the put-offs and put-ons needed for love in action. (Refer back to the chapter "Mocha Machines and other Weighty Stuff"). Make a battle plan for success. Hold yourself accountable to God, being encouraged when you succeed, forgiving yourself when you fail. It may take years, but victory will come as you focus on obedience. Rejoice as it does.
Action Tool:

- ❖ Get out the star chart and record a heart each day you successfully respond with love-in-action.
- ❖ Sometimes, at first, a whole day is too long. So, every time you are hungry and go to the refrigerator, record a heart for your successful loving response.
- ❖ Reward yourself with something sweet when you have 10 hearts.

Week 39, Day 4. Read: Romans 12:1–2.
Journal: How does today's scripture speak to you about your marriage? What is God's good, pleasing and perfect will for you today? Be specific.
Action Tool: Remember to do the star chart.

Week 39, Day 5. Read: Genesis 2: 22–23.

Journal: How in the years of your marriage have you and your husband become "one flesh"? How have you grown closer together in sharing, thinking, living, loving or walking with God? How has your husband shown his love to you?

Action Tool: Celebrate today the ways you have grown in love with a "toast" at dinner (use water or whatever). Share in your "toast" the qualities of "becoming one" the Lord revealed in your quiet time.

Slippery Rocks
Week 40, Day 1

> **Let us not become weary in doing good, for at the proper time we will reap a harvest if we do not give up.**
> **(Galatians 6:9)**

> Oh, my goodness, mist from Sweet Romance Falls creates a slippery slope! Be careful, gals, wouldn't want any twisted ankles. Climbing the steep path, a simple stumble on wet rocks could result in a dangerous fall. Keep watch, ladies.

I hear you crying, "You don't understand. My husband is so difficult. It's all about him. Consider my needs? No way! He is so self-centered." Wow, yours too? That sounds just like my husband. In fact, that sounds just like me. Let's face it; we are all self-centered, selfish humans. We want our own way more than anything else, plus throw in no pain or self-sacrifice either.

"OK, I got it," you say, "We are all selfish. But how does that help if I am laying down my life for my husband and he is not laying down his life for me? I am seeking to act loving. He is just lapping it up but giving nothing back. So, what do I do?" What does God say?

> Let us not become weary in doing good, for at the proper time we will reap a harvest if we do not give up. Therefore, as we have opportunity, let us do good to all people (our husband too), especially to those who belong to the family of believers.
>
> (Galatians 6:9–10)

Being a believer is not a magic love potion. A lifetime of obedience to His word transforms us, yet often we hear His word but do not act on it.

This may be true of your husband whether or not he is a Christian. When one stumbles on the slippery slope of selfishness, both the husband and wife may tumble injuring the marriage. Your job is to "not weary in well doing".

> God said it is possible to be loving when others are unloving. Therefore, it is possible, and He provides the strength to do so. Remember, "I can do all things though Christ who strengthens me."
>
> (Philippians 4:13)

Our responsibility is to be right before the Lord for our actions. What is God calling you to do in faithfulness to his word? It matters not how your husband responds; your choices need to reflect the Holy Spirit within you.

Continue to cover your husband in prayer, asking God to change his heart and actions. Count not on man's faithfulness but on God's. Meanwhile, seek new ways to show him your love. What actions speak love to him? Sex and food, of course. What else? Honor your husband as your hero. Anoint him with kind words.

Even if your husband changes, it will never be enough. He will always fall short. Instead of focusing on his shortcomings, focus on his praiseworthy qualities. You heard my story of pain with my husband so realize I speak from experience.

Catapulting off the rocks of selfishness breaks our bonds of love. Bruised, in pain and exhausted we yearn to quit.

> Even youths grow tired and weary, and young men stumble and fall; but those who hope in the Lord will renew their strength. They will soar on wings like eagles; they will run and not grow weary, they will walk and not be faint.
>
> (Isaiah 40:30–31)

To not be weary, we must go aside to our holy mountain, our garden, our quiet nook and be still with God. Bask in his word for comfort and wisdom. Seek a restful night of sleep. Relax on Sunday. Nourish yourselves with healthy food and exercise. Set aside time with Christian women who uplift, listen and laugh. Taking care of yourself is vital for well-being. If we are too hungry, angry, lonely, or tired we cannot stand strong.

HALT–Too Hungry, Angry, Lonely, Tired.

- ❖ Hungry – Man does not live by bread alone but by every word that come from the word of God. (Matthew 4:4)
- ❖ Angry – In your anger, do not sin; do not let the sun go down on your anger. (Ephesians 4:26)
- ❖ Lonely – Jesus says I will never leave you for forsake you. (Hebrews 13:5b)
- ❖ Tired – Come to me all ye who are weak and heavy laden, and I will give you rest for your souls. (Matthew 11:28–29)

You can change no one but yourself. Commit to pouring God's love through you to the unlovable (especially your husband and children). Do not concern yourself with the reactions of your husband. Instead, be an instrument of God, doing right in His eyes. Focus on being an encourager. Expect failure. Pick yourself up, brush off, pray, look up, trudge ahead.

Sisters in Christ, I cannot imagine living through the hard knocks of life without your encouragement. Need a boost, Kara? Watch it, Katie, that section is especially slippery. Yes, we are weary of this long trek, yet together we can do it!

Prayer: Lord, sometimes I am weary of doing good. I believe the lie that quitting will relieve the pain. Fly me above the problem. Enable me to view it with a Godly perspective. Provide strength to face another day. Pour out your love through me when I have none. Abba, help.

Hide in My Heart: "Let us not become weary in doing good, for at the proper time we will reap a harvest if we do not give up. Therefore, as we have opportunity, let us do good to all people (our husband too), especially to those who belong to the family of believers" (Galatians 6:9–10).

Choose Today: Even though I am weary, Lord, I will continue to seek you and keep on, keeping on, in your strength.

Week 40, Day 2. Reread: Galatians 6:9–10 and Isaiah 40:30–31.
Journal: Write HALT from today's teaching. Examine how these circumstances affects your ability to stay loving.
Action Tool: Act immediately to overcome weariness.
Week 40, Day 3. Read: Philippians 4:13.
Journal: Do you depend on your own strength during the day? How is that working for you? How can you access the strength of Christ during your day? Ask God for specific instruction.
Action Tool: Write on a card, "Yes, I can do this. Jesus is my strength." Read it often.

Week 40, Day 4. Read: Philippians 4:8–9.
Journal: Think through the times when you feel unloved by your husband. Are these times resulting from your selfishness, from over sensitivity, from misunderstanding, from impatience, or from unkindness on his part? How might you show love in this same circumstance? Not emotions but action love from 1 Corinthians 13.
Action Tool: Create a habit to pray throughout the day.

- Find a button, a marble, or another small object. Place it in your pocket.
- This button reminds you to pray for your husband and for yourself.
- When you change clothes, move the button to the new pocket.

Week 40, Day 5. Read: 2 Thessalonians 2:16–17, Proverbs 12:25.
Journal: From today's scripture, what has Jesus Christ and God the Father promised to do? In what? What word do we need to speak to our husband?
Joy Trail: Praise or compliment. Speak words of encouragement, praise and appreciation to your husband today.

Boundary Fence
Week 41, Day 1

> **There is a way that seems right to a man (woman), but its end is the way of death.**
> **(Proverbs 14:12)**

> Come ladies, over to this fence. Look down. See the mighty thundering of Sweet Romance Falls. Whoa, sure glad this iron fence is standing firm. It is a long way to the bottom.

God calls us to love, to sacrifice our life for others, to show patience and kindness. Yet, sometimes we get confused about how love differs from being a doormat, walked on, trodden with dirty boots, ignored and discarded. This is not God's plan! Yes, He calls us to love and forgive. However, God speaks volumes about setting boundaries which save one from plunging to death. Reread our title verse for today,

> There is a way that seems right to a man (woman), but its end is the way of death.
> (Proverbs 14:12)

Loved ones maybe locked into abusive behaviors. Their emotional responses or physical habits may destroy family members. Addictive behaviors blind them to the hurt they inflict on others. Addicts justify their actions with a plethora of excuses. They blame everyone else, resulting in put-downs, yelling, rage, hitting. Profuse apologies may occur but not a real change.

As their loving wife or parent, we may seek to *save* them from their destructive behaviors. We may scold, threaten, beg or cry. Often, we believe when told we are worthless and get hooked by their blame. We try harder, with extreme effort, to do better. We hope that maybe, if we do this or that, he will be different. But it does not work! Then we become bitter, fearful, depressed and self-destructive. This is not God's way.

Historically men treated women as property with no rights or respect. They traded daughters in marriage for land or money. God, however, created women from man 's side to be a helper by his side, not trodden under his foot. The Bible honor women as mothers, judges, businesswomen, and disciples. Jesus treated women as equals with men. (Equal doesn't mean the same job description.) Read Proverbs 31 for an excellent picture of a woman of God. Even though you are a "work in progress", you deserve respect. Accept nothing less.

God requires our children as well to honor their parents from birth to death. It is our job to be Godly parents, to treat our children with respect even in discipline. It is their responsibility to show us respect. Accept nothing less.

If we allow our spouse and children to abuse us; if we feel more responsibility for their life and choices than they do, we are crippling them. Perhaps, your husband or child is abusing you. The pain is unbearable. You desperately want to fix it or escape. You are disintegrating into a miserable, unhealthy woman. So, what to do?

- ❖ Be aware, scripture recommends boundaries against foolish, evil, abusive behaviors.
    - o A man's (woman's) own folly ruins his (her) life, yet his (her) heart rages against the Lord. (Proverbs 19:3)
    - o Better a meal of vegetables than a fatted calf with hatred. (Proverbs 15:17)
    - o Do not make friends with a hot-tempered man (woman), do not associate with one easily angered, or you may learn his (her) ways and get ensnared. (Proverbs 22:24–25)
    - o It is better to live on a corner of the roof than share a house with a quarrelsome wife (husband). (Proverbs 21:9)
- ❖ Understand what abuse is: "To attack by words, to misuse, to use so as to injure or damage, to deceive, physical maltreatment, vehemently expressed condemnation, verbal degradation." Webster's New Collegiate Dictionary

- ❖ The abusive person often exhibits a) intense blame on everyone else for his/her abuse, b) apology and grief over their abuse with a promise never to be this way again, c) rationalization that their lapse into abuse is your fault once again.

  A hot-tempered man (woman) must pay the penalty; if you rescue him (her), you will have to do it again.
  (Proverbs 19:19)

- ❖ Seek Godly Scripture-based council.
  - o The prudent see danger and takes refuge, but the simple keep going and suffer for it. (Proverbs 27:12)
  - o A victim of abuse needs help. She must grasp what is abusive in her relationship and how she buys into it. She requires insight into being an enabler or responding to abuse with abuse.
  - o The abused woman needs aid and support when deciding on boundaries. What limits for well-being need enforcing?
  - o The abusive person may get worse when their victim first ceases tolerating abuse. She may need to absent herself from the situation.
  - o Do not go it alone.
- ❖ Seek a prayer group of Christian sisters to uphold and support you.
- ❖ Evaluate your own behavior so you are "love in action" *despite* the abuse. You cannot be an instrument of healing if you succumb to *giving out* abusive behavior.

Remember, you are not responsible for his/her choices, only for your own. It is easy to become ugly and militant when first setting boundaries so we ourselves become abusive. It is much harder to stay loving and forgiving while making changes. Still, God says we can.

You are of great value and worth in the eyes of God. He knit you together in your mother's womb. Though you falter, He will enable you to stand strong and loving while accepting no less than respect from your loved ones. God will guide you in boundary actions or will give you refuge away from the abuse. Do not just live with it. Seek help. Run to the strong tower of the Lord.

> Being confident of this that he who began a good work in you will carry it on to completion until the day of Christ Jesus.
>
> (Philippians 1:6)

Setting boundaries for my family was difficult. Family members were stuck in verbal abusive behaviors. I reacted as a miserable wretch. My first boundary banned sarcasm. No sarcasm, ever! It is not funny; it is hurtful. No put-downs or antagonistic tone of voice. Tone of voice says everything. Conversation ended. "When you wish to talk without sarcasm, put-downs or that tone of voice, the conversation will resume. Meanwhile, I am absenting myself from this discussion." At first, the sarcasm and ugly words became louder and more intense but lost its punch with no audience. Funny thing, once my husband got-it, when I lost-it, he refused to accept an antagonistic voice from me. It worked!

> Just as this fence has kept us safe from falling, ladies, so families need boundary fences. Boundaries allow bad choices to reap natural consequences. Meanwhile, my job was to stay connected to the Lord and act in love. Difficult! But I did it. So, can you!

Prayer: Father God, you know it is hard for us to set boundaries. Show us the way to establish appropriate boundaries while holding out a hand of forgiveness and love. It seems impossible. I desperately need your miraculous intervention to handle this issue. Amen

Hide in My Heart: "The prudent see danger and takes refuge, but the simple keep going and suffer for it" (Proverbs 27:12).

Choose Today: I choose to make prudent decisions regarding abuse and seek refuge when necessary.

Week 41, Day 2. Read: Proverbs 27:12.
Journal: In prayer, examine abusive behavior between you and your spouse, parents, or children. What abusive strongholds passed from your

family of origin to your household? How do they manifest in your home? Pray for a strong conviction about the boundaries needed against this abuse. Pray for the ability to love and forgive these same people, even while they are yet locked in the abusive behavior.
Action Tool:

- ❖ Seek Godly scripture-based council.
- ❖ Plan boundaries.
- ❖ Seek to forgive and love by the power of God despite the troubles.

Week 41, Day 3. Read: Proverbs 19:19.
Journal: The abusive person often exhibits a) intense blame on everyone else for his/her abuse, b) apology and grief over their abuse with a promise never to be this way again, c) rationalization that the lapse is your fault. Is this a pattern in your home? Journal what the Lord reveals to you.
Action Tool:

- ❖ Discern what is *your responsibility* in a typical abusive incident in your home. Discern what is *not you*, therefore you need not own. Practice saying to yourself, "This is me; I accept it. That is not me, I will not own it."
- ❖ No physical abuse allowed, ever, for any reason. Physical abuse requires absenting yourself and your children from the abuser. If you are the abuser, it may require taking yourself out of the picture until you get help.

Week 41, Day 4. Read: Proverbs 10: 19, 12:18, 13:2–3.
Journal: Resist verbal abuse. Do not give or accept verbal put-downs, insults or sarcasm, even in tone of voice. If you are sarcastic or prone to putting others down, Stop It! If you are the recipient, do not accept put-down words into your being. Tell yourself, "That is their issue, not who I am." Journal examples, if applicable, of verbal abuse you, your husband, or children spew, hurting one another.
Action Tool: Inform family members you will no longer take part in conversations that include put-downs, sarcasm or nasty tone of voice. That hurtful words are banned. When put-downs or sarcasm occur, you

will STOP, U-TURN, and ABSENT YOURSELF until both of you can speak the truth in love.

Week 41 Day 5. Read: Proverbs 18:10, 16:24 and Philippians 1:6.
Journal: Run to the strong tower of God. Jesus can bring life out of death in relationships, if you are willing, if your spouse is willing. Decide on your places of refuge. For instance, walk away from verbal abuse to your quiet garden nook or a walk around the neighborhood. Go to a friend's home. Hide out, if necessary, at a gospel mission. Create a plan.
Action Tool:

- At the moment, tell yourself, "I am of great worth in God's sight. I do not deserve this treatment. I will not respond in kind."
- Visualize opening a large umbrella. The unkind words rain down on the umbrella, falling around you but never touching you.
- Then PRAY for love and forgiveness to flow forth from you while enforcing boundaries required.

Joy Trail: Drip-Off Put-Downs. When slanderous words rain on you, put up your umbrella and allow "put-downs" to drip off with nary a drop touching you. Say inside your head, "No thank you, that is not who I am, so, I will not accept it."

Sheltering Pines
Week 42, Day 1

> **Clothe yourselves with compassion, kindness, humility, gentleness and patience. Bear with each other and forgive whatever grievances you may have against one another. Forgive as the Lord forgave you. And over all these virtues put on love, which binds them all together in perfect unity.**
>
> **(Colossians 3: 12-14)**

> Heavens, what a torrent of rain. The sun shone a few minutes ago. Come, huddle under these dense pines away from the Boundary Fence. Don your rain ponchos, settle under the trees and let's talk about forgiveness.

When hurt, normal human behavior reacts with anger and hardness of heart. Be it a small snub or a major, irreparable incident, the hurt may fester, become infected and invade our entire being. It consumes our emotions, changing us from a Godly woman to a bitter hag. It is time, dear ones, to forgive. Remember this verse:

> The foolish woman tears her house (her inner self and everyone around her) down but a wise woman builds hers up.
>
> (Proverbs 14:1)

Look around you at the hatred and vengeance in our society, the lack of forgiveness. What fruits do you see?

> Then Peter came to Jesus and asked, "Lord, how many times shall I forgive my brother when he sins against me?

Up to seven times?" Jesus answered, "I tell you, not seven times, but seventy-seven times."

(Matthew 18:31)

He instructs us to forgive, again and again and again. Forgiveness is dreadfully hard without the power of God. Yet, He does not leave us helpless; He provides the ability to forgive. Align yourself with God. Be willing to forgive despite your current emotions. Pray to understand the pain experienced by the one who hurt you. Intercede for him/her. Wait upon God until a transformation occurs enabling you to release the hurt and forgive.

I will remove from them their heart of stone and give them a heart of flesh.

(Ezekiel 11:19b)

Why forgive? After all, they have wronged you and it hurt to the core. Your mind says, "He does not deserve forgiveness. He needs to pay for his hurtful behavior. If I forgive, he will just do it again. Besides, he isn't a bit repentant." Yes, that may be true, but God still calls us to forgive.

Bear with each other and forgive whatever grievances you may have against one another. Forgive as the Lord forgave you.

(Colossians 3:13)

Sometimes, we hold hurt close to our heart, cherishing it. We refuse to accept God's forgiveness of us, thus unwilling and unable to forgive others. We claim a right to our bitterness. While stuck in hard-heartedness, you become a victim of the person who hurt you. That person controls you. They may not know or *care*. Yet, thoughts of the wrong inflicted consumes you. It controls your emotions, giving the one who hurt you power over you. Forgiving another is for *you,* not for them! It frees you from the emotional burden. It enables clear thinking.

Do not seek revenge or bear a grudge against one of your people but love your neighbor as yourself.

(Leviticus 19:18)

Holding onto your bitterness towards another is like tying a sack of rocks around your feet and jumping into a shallow lake. Your head is above water, so no drowning. But the rocks trap you in the mud. Unable to swim, float, enjoy the lake, your frustration grows as you thrash about in anger and frustration. Forgiveness cuts the rope. Forgiveness regenerates life in you even though you may need to set boundaries to avoid future injury or separate yourself from abuse. Despite boundaries, hurt is inevitable, therefore, stand ready to forgive repeatedly. As Jesus did for us, forgive while they are yet unrepentant. God promises blessings for your obedience.

> Do not repay evil with evil, or insult with insult, but with blessing because to this you were called so that you may inherit a blessing.
>
> (1 Peter 3:9)

God will guide. Bitterness departs resulting in a quiet mind.

> Clothe yourselves with compassion, kindness, humility, gentleness and patience. Bear with each other and forgive whatever grievances you may have against one another. Forgive as the Lord forgave you. And over all these virtues put on love, which binds them all together in perfect unity. Let the peace of Christ rule in your heart, since as members of one body you were called to peace. And be thankful.
>
> (Colossians 3:12–15)

As you forgive, through the power of Jesus, it sets you free! Untie the rock sack. Go swimming, let love flow.

> Sisters, the squall is finished. Amazing how mountain thunderstorms appear and dump, followed by delicate sunlight filtered through glistening pine branches. Raindrops become shimmering diamonds; a forest of diamonds! God can transform your hurt into love if you allow it. What a wonder.

Prayer: Forgiving is so difficult, Lord. I forgive, then ugly memories pop up and bitterness takes over again. Take my reluctant mind and transform my attitude by your power. Enable me to let go completely. Amen

Hide in My Heart: "Forgive as the Lord forgave you. And over all these virtues put on love, which binds them all together in perfect unity," (Colossians 3: 13–14)

Choose Today: I choose to let go of my bitterness and forgive through the power of God Almighty.

Week 42, Day 2. Read: Ezekiel 11:19b.
Journal: Against whom do you hold a grudge? Journal how hardness of heart towards this person affects your relationship? Pray for willingness to forgive this person.. Write Ezekiel 11:19 in your journal. Claim this promise.
Action Tool: Take your hardness of heart seriously. Agree with God that bitterness is sin.

Week 42, Day 3. Read: Colossians 3:3–14.
Journal: After reading today's scripture, consider God's instruction when hurt. What boundaries are necessary for the situation? What forgiving actions?
Action Tool: Prepare a Put-Off/Put-On Battle Plan for forgiveness. Refer to chapter "Pack Mules".

Week 42, Day 4. Read: Matthew 18:21–31.
Journal: Harboring bitterness tears our house apart. Yet we grow weary of forgiving. Take this to the Lord. Ask for His guidance and strength.
Action Tool: Add a "Forgive" charm to your prayer bracelet or a button to your pocket that represents a person you need to forgive. Every time you notice the charm or button, shoot up a quick prayer.

Week 42, Day 5. Read: Proverbs 14:1 and 1 Peter 3:9.
Journal: Do you want God's blessing, or would you prefer to keep your bitterness? One or the other. Your choice. How does today's verse apply it to a specific situation?
Joy Trail: Forgiving sets you free to be better, not bitter. Call on God to enable you to forgive.

Love Lookout
Week 43, Day 1

> **Pleasant words are a honeycomb, sweet to the soul and healing to the bones.**
> **(Proverbs 16:24)**

> OK, hikers, behold the spectacular vista of the golden valley, majestic mountains, and cascading river from Love Lookout. "The heavens declare the glory of God; and the firmament shows His handiwork." (Psalm 19:1) He spoke this all into being!

My six-month-old Havanese puppy sits by my side gazing with adoring eyes. One word, her name, impels this little black and white fluffy ball to my lap, enthusiastically licking my face. One scolding word stops her. Though she does not yet understand my words, she recognizes my tone of voice and body language.

God spoke the world into being. What power! He gave us tremendous power with words. We cannot speak a frog or flower into being, yet we can create an ulcer or contentment by mere words.

> With the tongue we praise our Lord and Father, and with it we curse human beings, who have been made in God's likeness. Out of the same mouth come praise and cursing. My brothers and sisters, this should not be.
> (James 3:9–10)

Recently, I was reading a secular book* about the effects of hormones, serotonin and dopamine, on the human body. These are "feel good" hormones. Two points impacted me. First, a drug addict on heroin and a person falling profoundly in love have the same dopamine levels. They

---

* <u>The Honeymoon Effect</u> by Bruce H. Lipton, Ph.D. - HayHouse

experience the same euphoric high and the same devastating crash. The new lover experiences this high when near the loved one. The crash occurs due to separation, doubt, or a breakup.

Couples long in love, the book asserts, sustain adequate hormone levels to induce a comfortable love-filled well-being. The research reported dopamine and serotonin levels can rise to healthy, heart-warming, sustainable levels through *words!*

> A woman has joy by the answer of her mouth, and a word spoken in due season, how good it is!
> (Proverbs 15:23)

During the "falling in love" phase couples choose words carefully to foster the romance and excitement. Seeking return of our affection, intimate words that cherish, admire and uplift the loved one flow freely. Yet, after the honeymoon phase is over, we quench being "in-love" with critical words, forgetting to uplift one another. Our words frequently bring pain and sorrow. An emotional crash or slow growth away from the sense of being "in-love" results. Scripture advises care with speech.

> For the tongue has the power of life and death. The soothing tongue is a tree of life, but a perverse tongue crushes the spirit.
> (Proverbs 18: 21, Proverbs 15:4)

However, as the words of God bring life, so can ours! They can bring sweetness to the soul and healing to the bones! Through words we can create love everlasting in our relationships thus induce contentment and joy. A scientist discovered this, but God created it. Listen to His advice written over two-thousand years ago:

- o Pleasant words are a honeycomb, sweet to the soul and healing to the bones. (Proverbs 16:24)
- o Reckless words pierce like a sword, but the tongue of the wise (loving, uplifting words) brings healing. (Proverbs 12:18)
- o An anxious heart weights a man down, but a kind word cheers him up. (Proverbs 12:25)

o   Anxiety in the heart of man cause depression but a good word makes it glad. (Proverbs 12:25)

To enhance the serotonin and dopamine levels (God's gift of good feelings), in our relationship we must concentrate on whatever is good and excellent about our loved one. With an intentional effort speak those perceptions of goodness aloud.

> A cheerful look brings joy to the heart, and good news gives health to the bones.
>
> (Proverbs 15:30)

Get more than a little excited about this, ladies; this is amazing! Believe your words are powerful and effective. Pack up a basketful of *candy and cookie words* to pass out on every occasion. Become known as the woman with praise and encouragement on her lips. Not empty compliments, but heartfelt uplifting words specific for the hearer. This may take focused effort. Instead of spewing death, speak life.

> You are such an amazing group of women. When we started, I secretly grumbled over trekking this mountain again, but now I am so glad. Kara, what bravery hiking this mountain being pregnant and uncertain. Monica, thank you for sharing your heart with these pilgrims. Kathi, your wisdom and encouragement kept me writing. Stacy, you helped this vintage lady over the rough parts. Sisters, you enrich my life.

Prayer: Father, we did not realize our words have such power. Help, O Lord, to tame our tongue. Change us so words of life, not death, flow from our mouth. We are willing, Lord. Amen.

Hide in My Heart: "Pleasant words are a honeycomb, sweet to the soul and healing to the bones," (Proverbs 16:24).

Choose Today: I choose to become a woman of encouragement and praise starting today.

Week 43, Day 2. Reread: All scriptures from yesterday's lesson. Underline the value and effects of a well-spoken word of encouragement.
Journal: Copy the scriptures significant to you. Journal your thoughts.
Action Tool: List "pleasant words" words or phrases. Intentionally bestow several on someone each day.

Week 43, Day 3. Read: James 3:9–10 and Proverbs 18:21.
Journal: What habitual phrases do you speak? Listen to yourself for a day. Jot notes. Think about tone of voice? For example, exasperated, irritated, loud, disrespectful, or pleasant, encouraging, loving. What do you say when you are busy and impatient? When instructing or expressing a concern? List negative words, phrases or expressions you habitually use. For example, "That's stupid."
Action Tool: Recall the "No, No, Yes, Yes Tool" to remind you of how powerful words can be. (Found in Week 26, Grumbling Gulch.)

Week 43, Day 4. Read: Ephesians 4:29.
Journal: Short-tempered or unkind words often stem from habit or stress. Stowing or lashing out does not heal. Awareness, practice, time and prayer will reform your speech.
Action Tool: Using the negative habitual word list from yesterday, write a less charged and opposite word for each negative word or phrase. Avoid "You are…" phrases.

> Example 1. Smart versus Stupid
> Example 2. "A smart girl like you will work this out," versus, "You are stupid. That was dumb."
> Example 3. "Oh my, Honey. How are you feeling about being pregnant? What are your plans?" Versus, "You are stupid to get pregnant."

One way speaks hurt, the other speaks healing. Write your own examples of using constructive, healing words.

Week 43, Day 5. Reread: Proverbs 16:24.
Journal: Think being in love… think joy in being together… think delight in your husband… think strong hero. What phrases would be meaningful to him. For example, "Honey, I was thinking, if I was in danger, you would risk your life to save me. You are my protector. I love you for that." Work on truthful characteristics to affirm about your husband. Drop these sentences into the conversation at random. If he asks you why these comments, say, "Oh, I don't know. Just thinking how much I value and appreciate you." (Keep this lesson a secret. It will mean more to him.)
Action Tool: When affirming words are spoken to us we often internally refute them. Negative words we gather to our self, holding them close, while we allow positive words to bounce off. It is important to *absorb* instead the *positive words* spoken to you. Affirm the giver by saying, "Thank you, I appreciate your encouragement."

Dark Forest
Week 44, Day 1

> **Come, let us drink deep of love till morning; let us enjoy ourselves with love! For my husband is not at home... With persuasive words she led him astray; she seduced him with her smooth talk. All at once he followed her like an ox going to the slaughter.**
>
> **(Proverbs 7:18–22)**

> I do love a romantic novel. Ah, what happens next in this sultry scene? Does he betray his wife? Strip naked and have sex? Describe every intimate moment? Seductive dark ways deep in the forest where no sunlight touches. Oh, my.

Our God created sex for procreation, pleasure and oneness between a husband and wife.

> May your fountain be blessed, and may you rejoice in the wife of your youth. A loving doe, a graceful deer, may her breast satisfy you always, may you ever be captivated by her love.
>
> (Proverbs 5: 18-19)

God intentionally glues a man and woman together with the natural irresistible act of sexual love. Of course, our fallen world has corrupted sexual love making it a casual commodity. Throughout history, Godly women, preserved the standard of purity, modesty and appropriate, God ordained sexuality. We women, not the men. Put men in a mining camp away from women, with rare exceptions, (historical facts state) are a bawdy, degenerated, immoral lot.

Increasingly though, women, even those with a desire to follow our Lord, have seared our minds with unrighteous reading and viewing. Scar tissue forms preventing us from seeing immorality and impurity as tragic, painful and destructive. An alarming number of young women (teens through thirties), even in our churches, are addicted to internet pornography. Many women of all ages read romantic novels or magazines (Cosmopolitan) which are the equivalent of porn. Addiction to non-sexually graphic (soft) romantic novels may also consume and lead a woman astray.

> The eye is the lamp of the body. If your eyes are healthy, your whole body will be full of light.
> (Matthew 6:22)

One evening watching a movie with our house guest, (A Christian woman from another country who had rarely been exposed to television) I was startled when she gasped out loud. Her eyes were wide, her hands over her mouth. What was she seeing that caused such a reaction? To me, nothing much, just a man's feet and pants down in a toilet stall behind a door. To her it was obscene and inappropriate. She asked me to turn the movie off for she did not wish to poison her thoughts. Oh my, I realized that with so much filth in everyday TV, I became numb to what seemed minor in comparison. I thought my standards were high, but I was convicted, not high enough. My desire for entertainment is often stronger than my desire for righteousness.

As newlyweds, my husband asked me to set aside reading romantic novels. Addicted, I read three gentle Christian romance novels each week. At that time, we struggled desperately in our marriage. He realized I compared him to fictional Godly men. This increased my disgruntled opinions of him. He unveiled my escaped to fantasy men. And he was right! The fantasy felt good, away from my unhappy reality. This idolatry drew me away from my husband and my God.

How does sexual impurity in our minds affect our joy? Let's return to Solomon's instruction to the young men. It is the same for women, be it physical or mental adultery.

> Like an ox going to the slaughter, like a deer stepping into a noose, till an arrow pierces his liver, like a bird darting into a snare, little knowing it will cost him his life. Listen to me, pay attention to what I say. Do not let your heart (mind, eyes) turn to her ways (reading, viewing, following) or stray to her paths (dress, speech, actions). Many are the victims she has brought down; her slain are a mighty throng. Her house (books, movies, porn, actions) are a highway to the grave, leading down to the chambers of death.
>
> (Proverbs 7:22–27)

The harlot is loud and rebellious. She prefers night, sexy dress, wandering from home, is salacious, aggressive, seeks male company. She speaks with enticement and flattery. Modeling harlot type behavior is acceptable in the world's club while modeling modesty and righteousness are ridiculed and abhorred.

> The wicked freely strut about when what is vile is honored by the human race.
>
> (Psalm 12:8)

Death is the result. Something good becomes rotten. Are your choices in media, books, speech, dress and actions reflecting purity or do they reflect that which is sexual and profane? Are you escaping your pain through indulging in entertainment or attention that is abhorrent to our God? If we quench the Holy Spirit by our choices, we also quench our joy and peace with God.

> For though we live in the world, we do not wage war as the world does. The weapons we fight with are not the weapons of the world. On the contrary, they have divine power to demolish strongholds. We demolish arguments and everything that sets itself up against the knowledge of God, and we take captive every thought to make it obedient to Christ.
>
> (2 Corinthians 10:3–5)

Be honest, we have been seduced by media, fashion, and our own sexual appetites. Sexual enticement is tempting and does not appear to hurt. After all, it is just a movie. No, do not believe the sugar-coated lie of Satin. It is time to turn around and seek life-giving purity. Let us be different from the world. Become a woman who models God's standard of purity, modesty and appropriate, God ordained, sexuality.

> The "Dark Forest" path looks easier than the "Narrow Trail". The wildflowers and blackberries entice us to wander in that direction. Heaven forbid! Once a group of us ladies tried the Dark Forest path. What a mistake. Believe me, the lovely meadow grew dark and forbidding. Dense trees suffocated the foliage and choked out the sun. In the dismal dankness the trail petered out. We turned around, scurried back to the sunlight, and proceeded on the steep "Narrow Trail". God grants compassion on our wayward journeys into impurity. He forgives, then escorts us back to Godliness, if we are willing.

Prayer: Must I give up pleasure, Lord? No, you created pleasure. I understand. I must give up everything that masquerades as pleasure but instead destroys. Forgive me, but the devil seems so much louder and more prolific that you God. Sexual temptation is so enticing and pervasive. Open my eyes to truth and light by your power and grace, O Lord. Amen.
Hide in My Heart: "The eye is the lamp of the body. If your eyes are healthy, your whole body will be full of light," (Matthew 6:22)
Choose Today: I choose to examine my media and thought content, my attire and flirtatiousness so that my choices come into alliance with the word of God. Lord help.

Week 44, Day 2. Read: Galatians 5:5–9.
Journal: Pray for yourself and/or family members locked in sexual addictions (movies, explicit books, internet porn, or promiscuity).
Action Tool: Listen to truth rather than lies. Turn off, prohibit, block and remove from your home that which is profane. Flee.

Week 44, Day 3. Read: Matthew 6:22.
Journal: What is your escape from reality into a false pleasure? Do you comfort yourself with habits that sear your mind? What have you sowed that reaps unhealthy or ungodly consequences? Ask the Lord to convict you of compromise in which you indulge. Pray for victory so that your body will be full of light.
Action Tool: Rubber band snap: Wear a wide rubber band or a rubber bracelet. When your thoughts are tempted to stray, snap the band and say, "I can do all things through Christ who strengthens me." The tiny bit of irritation from the snap is a reminder to focus on the Lord.

Week 44, Day 4. Read: 2 Corinthians 10:3–5.
Journal: Remember, you do not walk this road alone. God already forgave you for your transgressions through Jesus Christ. Saved from sin by grace alone, through faith alone, in Christ alone. He works within you to renew your mind and habits. So, no guilt trips, just one step forward. Journal your next step as God guides.
Action Tool: Fall on your knees. Claim just for today, with the power of God, I will not go there!

Week 44, Day 5. Read: 1 Peter 3:1–5.
Journal: Consider your clothing. Does it honor God? Styles and coverings vary with generations and cultures, but God's word is the standard by which to judge. Is your clothing designed to entice men or to reveal a quiet beauty? In what way might you need change?
Action Tool: Scripting of the world says, "Feeling sexy equals looking good, equals feeling good." See this "sexy script" as a lie. A beautiful spirit graced by lovely clothes that exemplify modesty is God's way. Sexy is for your husband.

Wild Honeysuckle
Week 45, Day 1

> **Many waters cannot quench love; rivers cannot wash it away.**
>
> **(Song of Songs 8:7)**

> Girls, what a heavenly fragrance from that wild honeysuckle bush. The sweet fragrance of lovers in love, at some point, becomes the deep musky scent of intimate sexual fulfillment. As mentioned before, this was God's intent. Sexual intercourse glues a man and a woman together creating oneness. Unfortunately, sex as a casual commodity loses its stickiness. Yet, as with everything else under the sun, God is the master of redemption.

> For this reason, a man will leave his father and mother and be united to his wife, and the two will become one flesh?
>
> (Matthew 19:5)

The world dwells on sex. Christian women seldom mention it. The Bible, though, speaks openly. Our God created sex and said it was good, so let's boldly discuss how to grow as a Godly sexual woman. Blessed to live in this century and country, women are free to express their sexuality. Even so, we must filter our expression through the word of God.

The physical act of intercourse results in a union of the body and communion of the mind. God designed this communication with our body to be tender and fulfilling for both the husband and wife. A couple long married, deeper in love today than on their wedding day, exemplify God's plan.

> May your fountain be blessed, and may you rejoice in the wife of your youth. A loving doe, a graceful deer, may her breast satisfy you always, may you ever be captivated by her love.
>
> (Proverbs 5:18–19)

Many couples experience a brokenness in their sexual union. A history of promiscuity, abusive sex, selfish interactions, lack of loving concern, and weariness dissolve the glue. For a renewed mind and enjoyment in lovemaking with your husband, put the past behind you. Move forward anticipating something good. Where to begin? Embrace that God created sex, not the world. Within the confines of marriage, God designed it for delight and comfort.

Men react quickly to sexual stimulus and may have little regard for female emotions. Women prefer a slow warm glow as a pathway to intimacy. Conflict often results. Childbirth, child rearing, work, menopause, cooking, housecleaning also interfere with a woman's desire. Sex becomes another job required at the end of a weary day. Not quite what we have in mind but sometimes necessary. Doesn't feel like oneness. It feels like being used.

So, take responsibility, girlfriends, for your own feelings. Instead of turning off, turn around. Spontaneity is great when you are both available and aroused but often life interferes. Remember, you cannot change your husband. You can only change yourself. As you become God's specially designed playmate for your husband, he may reciprocate as a more loving mate. If not, then as with all other circumstances, God will bless you for your loving actions.

So, here is a plan to consider:

- ❖ Pray for insight regarding your sexual relationship with your husband. Consider what is arousing for you... the environment, scents, sound, clothes, and touch.
- ❖ Over coffee, ask your husband what appeals to him... the environment, scents, sound, clothes, and touch.

- Again, over coffee not in bed, explain what excites you sexually. Telling him you prefer a certain touch is less ego deflating when not amid lovemaking. Be aware, much embarrassing trial and error may occur before you become amazing lovers. Or it may come naturally and all you require is a special time for loving. Either way, do not get upset or disappointed if your plans go astray. Performance anxiety can wreak havoc for men and turn off women completely. Don't give up. Try again another day.
- Take charge of planning romantic events, separate from the rollover in bed moments. Do not leave it up to him. Plan what appeals to you, the woman. Toss in what appeals to him. Make it a date (an appointment you are asking him to keep). Have the children elsewhere.
- Tell your husband a hint of what to expect. Expectation enhances arousal. Give him an idea of your expectations since he cannot read your mind. Maybe mail a perfumed note several days in advance.
- Make it fun. Something to anticipate.

A paraphrase of I Corinthians 7:2-6 by <u>The Message</u> speaks to our sexuality so well:

> It's good for a man to have a wife, and for a woman to have a husband. Sexual drives are strong, but marriage is strong enough to contain them and provide for a balanced and fulfilling sexual life in a world of sexual disorder. The marriage bed must be a place of mutuality—the husband seeking to satisfy his wife, the wife seeking to satisfy her husband. Marriage is not a place to "stand up for your rights." Marriage is a decision to serve the other whether in bed or out. Abstaining from sex is permissible for a period if you both agree to it, and if it's for the purposes of prayer and fasting—but only for such times. Then come back together again.
>
> (1 Corinthians 7:2–6. The Message)

Cover your sexual life with prayer. Any hurts, disappointments or resentments requires prayer. Seek a solution that will set you free. What do you need to feel safe, open and ready for intimacy? If your husband lacks all sensitivity, is uncommunicative and uncooperative, ask God how to love despite your husband's attitude. Pray for sweet intimacy. Clothe yourself with forgiveness for your husband's ego frailty in this arena.

If your intimate relationship with your husband is fantastic, celebrate it. Make time to enjoy one another; do not let the flame go dim. Make the time!

With all the chaos in our home, Gene and I intentionally got away together once a quarter for a weekend. In between, I sent our children to a sitter and stayed home with special plans. My attention during daily life, did not focus on Gene, so quickies were routine. Planned events rekindled the romance or built it anew when painful struggles threatened to destroy our desire.

One of my girls recently asked, "Do you guys still make love now you are old?" My answer, "All the time. More than we ever did before."

"Whoa," she said, "Not sure I want to hear about this."

"You asked," I responded, chuckling. "We cuddle, kiss, touch, share our thoughts, laugh, and tease, hold hands, walk, and hug and serve one another. We are far more intimate now. It is all sexual and lovemaking, but not necessarily intercourse." This is the hard-earned oneness that grows out of communication and physical intimacy. God planned this for lovers from the beginning. We are fortunate, after thirty-five years of marriage, to have this blessing of the Lord.

> Sweet memories of the times away together enhance our conversations today. The first night on our retreats, we just debunked from daily stress. The second night involved fun, laughter, good food, and whatever came next. Now you know all my secrets. Ummm, I love the honeysuckle fragrance. So romantic!

Prayer: Oh, my goodness, another thing to consider, Lord. Must I? Can't I avoid the whole subject and let happen what happens? Convict me, God of Creation, if I need to change in this aspect of my life. Help me celebrate our oneness physically. Give me your heart for my husband. Thank you, God, for the beauty of sexuality between husband and wife. Amen.
Hide in My Heart: "My beloved spoke and said to me, "Arise, my darling, my beautiful one, come with me." "My beloved is mine and I am his." (Song of Songs 2:10, 2:16a).
Choose Today: Growing closer to my husband in body and understanding is on my mind today. Show me the way, Lord.

Week 45, Day 2. Reread: 1 Corinthians 7:2–6.
Journal: Bring your sexuality before the Lord. Carefully consider what is arousing for you… the environment, scents, sound, clothes, and touch. Also, consider what turns you off… environment, time of day, stress, and touch. *Do not expect your husband to "divine" these things.* You must tell him and not during love making. Over coffee, ask your husband what appeals most to him… the environment, scents, sound, clothes, and touch.
Action Tool: Make an appointment with your husband to talk about sex. Explain this discussion is not for criticism but to explore what you both enjoy. Pray for God's intercession in this conversation, especially if sexual discussion is awkward for either of you.

Week 45, Day 3. Read: The Song of Songs 7:10–13.
Journal: Be aware, much discussion and embarrassing trial and error may occur to learn what pleases your mate. Don't give up. Journal what the Lord has spoken to your heart from The Song of Songs.
Action Tool: Be ready to forgive and let go if your efforts go sour. Cover your disappointment in prayer and forgiveness.

Week 45, Day 4. Read: Matthew 19:5.
Journal: If you prepare an accepting attitude and say "Yes" regularly to a quickie, he will be more gracious on "No" nights. Still, to remain captivating, plan special times set apart for romance. Take charge of planning romantic times. Do not leave it up to him. Have the children elsewhere or steal a weekend away. Take time to plan a "secret tryst".

Action Tool: Get out your calendar. Secure an appointment for a playdate. Make it fun.

Week 45, Day 5. Read: Song of Songs 2:10 and 2:16a.
Journal: Journal what you expect of a romantic interlude. Think it through in advance. For example: You would like him to come home from work on time and take a shower. Start with kisses and hugs at the door, then gradually warm up with touch during dinner. Tell him what to anticipate from you. It will turn him on and you too. Write an enticing note.
Action Tool: Go buy a card or note paper. Write your note. Dab it with perfume. Hide it in his pocket, place on his pillow or visor, drop it in the mail. Pair it with a candy kiss.

Broken Bridge
Week 46, Day 1

> **Learn to be content whatever the circumstances. We know what it is to be in need, and we know what it is to have plenty. We must learn the secret of being content in any and every situation, whether well fed or hungry, whether living in plenty or in want. I can do all this through him who gives me strength.**
>
> **Philippians 4:11b-13**

> The Meadow of Gladness awaits, gals, across the bridge. Whoa! A storm destroyed the bridge. The Forest Service usually repairs winter damage by now, but I heard funds were short. Lord, we need an alternate way across the river.

Money, money, money - never enough, comes in, flies out. Money is a resource for pleasure and a source of woe. The Bible mentions money 140 times, plus additional references to riches and gold. Statistics list "fights over money" as the second most frequent issue for divorce. Even couples who have more than enough, may have vastly different attitudes towards spending. Have you ever argued over finances or worried about how to pay a bill? Then join the club. Let's dig in and discover God's prescription for relieving pain induced by money.

> Two things I ask of you, Lord; do not refuse me before I die: Keep falsehood and lies far from me; give me neither poverty nor riches but give me only my daily bread. Otherwise, I may have too much and disown you and say, "Who is the Lord?" or I may become poor and steal, and so dishonor the name of my God.
>
> (Proverbs 30:7–9)

We think having more money will solve our problems. A little more and we will be fine. This lie of the devil throws us off balance. Yes, we need sustenance. Yet beyond our daily bread, our greatest need is love and vitality for life. If our "attitude" towards finances is aligned with God's word, we can rest in Jesus and...

> Learn to be content whatever the circumstances. We know what it is to be in need, and we know what it is to have plenty. We must learn the secret of being content in any and every situation, whether well fed or hungry, whether living in plenty or in want. I can do all this through him who gives me strength.
>
> (Philippians 4:11b–13)

As always, easier said than done. I inherited a fear of insufficient income from my parents, who suffered through the losses of Great Depression and World War II. My husband and I agree on spending, so live frugal on daily expenses, yet generous within our means on vacations. So far, so good. Still, as we approached retirement, my subconscious fear drove me to strive for increased income. Through real-estate investment, we over-extended our finances.

When the real estate market crashed in 2008, we suffered great financial loss. We lost our home in the California wine country where we raised our family. We lost the rental units we purchased and our retirement IRA's. We moved into a camper parked on the back lot of a friend's farm. My health deteriorated due to the stress. Eventually, we had to go bankrupt. The day we filed bankruptcy, the courts allowed us $140 cash and a cottage in Idaho (one of our former rentals claimed as our residence). Now we lived in a strange town with no friends, family or jobs, bad health, and over sixty. Oh my!

Scripture does not promise wealth. In fact, wealth is a moving target based on the decade, country, and town. If you have more than your neighbor, you are wealthy to him. Gods concern is our "attitude", our willingness to trust Him, to work diligently and to use His provisions with wisdom and generosity.

God's word has input on all aspects concerning money:

So where is your pain connected with finances?

Not enough to pay the bills

> Therefore, I tell you, do not worry about your life, what you will eat or drink; or about your body, what you will wear. Is not life more than food, and the body more than clothes? Look at the birds of the air; they do not sow or reap or store away in barns, and yet your heavenly Father feeds them. Are you not much more valuable than they? Can any one of you by worrying add a single hour to your life?
>
> (Matthew 6:24–34)

Disagreement on how to handle finances

> Better a little with the fear of the Lord than great wealth with turmoil.
>
> (Proverbs 15:16)

Job loss

> In their heart humans plan their course, but the Lord establishes their steps.
>
> (Proverbs 16:9)

Employment

> Those who work their land will have abundant food, but those who chase fantasies will have their fill of poverty.
>
> (Proverbs 28:19)

> A little sleep, a little slumber, a little folding of the hands to rest—and poverty will come on you like a thief and scarcity like an armed man.
>
> (Proverbs 24:33–34)

Overextended on credit

> The rich rule over the poor, and the borrower is a slave to the lender.
>
> (Proverbs 22:7)

What attitudes do you harbor about money?

Compulsive spender

> Be sure you know the condition of your flocks (how your money is spent) ... for riches do not endure forever.
>
> (Proverbs 27:23a-24a)

Tightwad

> Whoever loves money never has enough; whoever loves wealth is never satisfied with their income. This too is meaningless.
>
> (Ecclesiastics 5:10)

Stingy

> A generous person will prosper; whoever refreshes others will be refreshed.
>
> (Proverbs 11:25)

Greed

> A greedy man brings trouble to his family.
>
> (Proverbs 15:27)

Envious

> A heart at peace gives life to the body, but envy rots the bones.
>
> (Proverbs 14:30)

> Keep your lives free from the love of money and be content with what you have, because God has said, "Never will I leave you; never will I forsake you."
>
> (Hebrews 13:5)

Lazy

> A sluggard's appetite is never filled, but the desires of the diligent are fully satisfied.
>
> (Proverbs 13:4)

Compulsive-obsessive worker

> Do not wear yourself out to get rich; do not trust your own cleverness. Cast but a glance at riches, and they are gone, for they will surely sprout wings and fly off to the sky like an eagle.
>
> (Proverbs 23:4–5)

> For the love of money is a root of all kinds of evil. Some people, eager for money, have wandered from the faith and pierced themselves with many griefs.
>
> (1 Timothy 6:10)

Blaming

> Starting a quarrel is like breaching a dam; so, drop the matter before a dispute breaks out.
>
> (Proverbs 17:14)

Giving

> Bring the whole tithe into the storehouse that there may be food in my house. "Test me in this," says the Lord Almighty, "and see if I will not throw open the floodgates of heaven and pour out so much blessing that there will not be room enough to store it."
>
> (Malachi 3:10)

Apply the word of God to your financial life. Invest in a Christian course on budgeting.

Meanwhile, evaluate your weaknesses regarding money. Seek to be content in your current financial circumstance, with no increase. Here are practical suggestions to get you started.

1. Pray with your husband over major purchases. Seek agreement in the Lord before deciding.
2. Think through each purchase, small or large, with the criteria, "Will this expenditure increase the *quality of our life?*" If the answer is, "No", then do not buy it.
3. Tithe. Even if you are financially struggling, learn to be generous by setting aside the first 10% of your income to "Give Away". *Be frugal in living, generous in giving.*
4. Trust and Save. Put the second 10% into savings/investments. Trust in the Lord for tomorrow while being diligent to work today.
5. Have an amount allocated for "Fun Money". Even a little saved up for something special gives freedom to splurge.
6. Plan in January for a vacation that year. Our bodies need time aside from daily life to rest and reconnect with family. *Make your vacation a priority, not an option.* Do what you can afford and stay within God's provision.
7. Be accountable to each other regarding finances. Walking in the light helps both husband and wife stay within their means.
8. View financial losses or your poor financial decisions, as expensive seminars from the hand of God.

If your husband is unwilling to work with you on financial changes, surrender his attitudes. Do not rescue him by usurping God's discipline over him. God may allow consequences to bring you both into alignment with His provision. Pray about this daily. Meanwhile, work on yourself. Surrender your attitudes and habits to Jesus, growing in wisdom and victory against your own money strongholds. Your husband may see the change in you resulting in better financial health for the family. This may open him to change. Most of all, count not on man's faithfulness, but on God's faithfulness even in finances.

In our financial loss, my husband announced as we set out for Idaho, "Gene and Anne's Great Adventure". With his forgiveness and upbeat attitude, despite his own anxiety, healing began. Old age poverty, my fear, became a reality. Yet, we never lacked for necessities. Thrift stores decorated our new home. Once a month fast-food dining was a treat. Determined to avoid bitterness at God and to be content despite the circumstances, I fought the depression. Turning to my Lord and strength, I claimed His abundance no matter our finances. I counted my blessings, praising His name, every morning and night. Gene and I continue to work in our old age. It keeps our minds alert and enables us to recoup. Our life is good. Seven years have passed. My heart rests regarding our finances. God is faithful even when He allows hard times.

> Ok, follow Stacy to that log jam, God provided a bridge! Cross over on that big old fallen tree. Young gals walk carefully using your staffs for balance. As for me, I am scooting on my hind end. Monica, will you give everyone a hand when they reach the other side. Thanks, Sweetie.

Prayer: Father, guide us as we tackle the stronghold of financial attitudes. We get possessive of "our" money. It is very hard to yield and trust. Our lust of stuff and fear of lack often compels poor money decisions. Please reveal our personal strongholds. Help us carry out change. In Jesus' name. Amen.

Hide in My Heart: "But godliness with contentment is great gain. For we brought nothing into the world, and we can take nothing out of it. But if we have food and clothing, we will be content with that," (1 Timothy 8:8).

Choose Today: Today I choose to adopt God's perspective on my attitude about money.

Week 46, Day 2. Reread: Proverbs 30:7–9.

Journal: Pray for insight into your own money issue strongholds. Ask the Lord to give you guidance for a Godly attitude and self-control.

Action Tool: Make an appointment with your husband to discuss finances from a God perspective.

Week 46, Day 3. Read: Go over the scripture bullet points from this week's lesson about money.
Journal: Note the issues on which you need to work. Write the verses in your journal which help convict or guide you.
Action Tool: Plan to tithe and save from the moment you get a paycheck, not from what is left over at the end of the month.

Week 46, Day 4. Read: Matthew 6:24–34.
Journal: Go over each step of practical application in the lesson. Note the steps you need to implement.
Action Tool: Decide on a sum for "Fun Money" that works within your means. Schedule dates, getaways and a vacation that works with your finances using the "Fun Money" set aside.

Week 46, Day 5. Read: 1 Timothy 6:10.
Journal: How does viewing your financial mistakes as "Instructive Seminars" improve your quality of life? These seminars teach from experience. How would contentment in all circumstances create a more abundant life?
Action Tool: Think, "Will this purchase, expenditure, increase the quality of our life?" If the answer is, "No," then do not buy it.

Sunrise Glory
Week 47, Day 1

She who pursues righteousness and love finds life.
(Proverbs 21:21a)

> Morning Ladies. What an incredible sunrise over the meadow! Shades of pink and gold crowning the brilliant orb rising above the meadow, framed by woods. A kiss of God for our day.

It is easy to share and grow close when life is gold and rosy. Yet, sometimes we criticize our nearest and dearest with every breath. As their negative qualities loom before us, we become blinded to their wonderful qualities. For the sake of love, today we focus on exalting one we love. It may be your spouse, or perhaps a child or sister. We call this person "the chosen one" as we embark on cultivating joy in this relationship.

Cultivating joy enhances both healthy and ailing relationships. If locked in dislike, anger, or despair over your chosen one, do not dismay. Despite the troubles you are experiencing, good and precious qualities exist. God can reveal these to you. It may be painful for you to concentrate on the good when you are hurting, so bathe these days in prayer. Ask for His guidance.

Be inspired, once again, by this verse:

> Finally, brothers and sisters, whatever is true, whatever is noble, whatever is right, whatever is pure, whatever is lovely, whatever is admirable—if anything is excellent or praiseworthy—think (dwell) about such things.
> (Philippians 4:8)

Seven Days of Cultivating Joy in A Relationship

Instructions: Select a "chosen one". <u>Choose a word label</u> to describe the quality for the day. <u>Dwell</u> on this quality, thinking how much you value this in him/her. <u>Expand</u> your thinking to moments in the past when this quality was exhibited. <u>Note</u> how that made you feel. <u>Pray scripture</u> for your chosen one. Remember, if negatives invade your thoughts, redirect your thinking. Tell yourself, "Thank you for sharing but, please, today share only good moments."

Label, dwell, expand, note and pray.

Day 1 Appreciation: List a characteristic you appreciate about the chosen one. Pray – Ephesians 1:16.

Day 2 Come out to Play: List a moment in time when you and the chosen one laughed together, enjoyed a favorite activity together, or just had pure fun with one another. Label, dwell, expand, note and pray. Pray – Proverbs 17:22.

Day 3 Beauty is in the Eye of the Beholder: List a physical characteristic you like about the chosen one. How does this quality make you smile? How has he/she used this physical quality to bring you joy. (i.e.: Lovely hands bringing you a cup of coffee.) Pray – Ephesians 3:17-19.

Day 4 Giving and Receiving: List a way your chosen one expresses his/her respect, friendship and love to you. Dwell and expand on real moments in time when you were the recipient of this expression of caring. Pray – Ephesians 5:22–33.

Day 5 Communication: List a communication attribute you appreciate about the chosen one. (i.e.: Willingness to talk, willingness to listen.) If poor communication exists, pray for insight. Persist until you find two positive aspects. If your mind bombards you with negatives, remember to say, "Thank you, self, for sharing but today, please, offer the good moments only." Label, dwell, expand, note and pray. Pray – Proverbs 20:5.

Day 6 Encourage: List a way *you* currently encourage and uplift the chosen one. If you find yourself lacking in this area, then pray for guidance in how you might become more adept at encouragement. Pray – Ephesians 1:17.

Day 7 Celebrate the Friendship: List three ways to delight the chosen one. Focus on his/her interests. Plan specific moments or activities. Anticipate the fulfillment. Plan, then execute the plan. Pray – Romans 12:12, 15:4.

Example 1: Quality – Appreciation

- ❖ Label the quality I appreciate—Loyalty
- ❖ Dwell—I have no fear that my husband will leave me or have an affair.
- ❖ Expand—He talks openly about temptations and places solid boundaries such as not spending time alone (behind closed doors) with other women, even at work.
- ❖ Note—This quality helps me feel relaxed and trusting in our marriage.
- ❖ Pray Scripture—Lord, motivate my husband daily to "Put on the full armor of God, so that he can take your stand against the devil's schemes," (Ephesians 6: 11).

Alternate Example 2: Quality – Appreciation

- ❖ Label the quality I appreciate—Strength
- ❖ Dwell—I know my Gene would risk his life for me if needed.
- ❖ Expand—When I fell down a hill through thorny bushes landing on my face, Gene plowed through the bushes, ignoring his own cuts and scrapes, to rescue me.
- ❖ Note—My hero, my protector. This quality causes me to feel proud and safe.
- ❖ Pray Scripture—I pray that my husband, "Being rooted and established in love, may have power, together with all the Lord's holy people, to grasp how wide and long and high and deep is the love of Christ, and to know this love that surpasses

knowledge—that he may be filled to the measure of all the fullness of God," (Ephesians 3: 17–19).

If you are struggling in your relationship, this exercise should be private, not shared with the loved one. Our conscious mind is quick to notice the negatives and ignore the positives. For this exercise, do not allow negatives. This is important. For seven days, focus on the characteristics you enjoy and appreciate in the chosen one.

With prayer and trust in our Lord, this tool provides an opportunity to speak life into our relationships. Take heart, rest in Jesus and focus on whatever is excellent.

"She who pursues righteousness and love finds life"
(Proverbs 21:21a)

What a magnificent day! We discovered joy while walking in the meadow, finding alpine flowers, making orange soda from the natural soda springs, and discovering the tiny hummingbird nest. To top it off, the purple and orange sunset was beyond description! So glad we took time to notice and dwell on whatever is excellent! Ahhh!

Prayer: Author of Love, Creator of Families, Father God, we ask your blessing on our adventure of cultivating joy in our relationships. Guide us in the unique way we can bless our chosen one with words, thoughts, and actions of love. Amen.

Start Today! Seven Days of Cultivating Joy in A Relationship.
Day 1 Appreciate: Refer to lesson.

Week 47, Day 2. Read: 1 Corinthians 13:1–3.
Day 2 Come out to Play: Refer to lesson.

Week 47, Day 3. Read: 1 John Chapter 1.
Day 3 Beauty is in the Eye of the Beholder: Refer to lesson.

Week 47, Day 4. Read: 1 John Chapter 2.
Day 4 Giving and Receiving: Refer to lesson.

Week 47, Day 5. Read: 1 John Chapter 3.
Day 5 Communication: Refer to lesson.

Week 47, Day 6. Read: 1 John Chapter 4.
Day 6 Encourage: Refer to lesson.

Week 47, Day 7. Read: 1 John Chapter 5.
Day 7 Celebrate the Friendship: Refer to lesson.

Meadow of Gladness
Week 48, Day 1

> **She who heeds the word wisely will find good, and whoever trusts in the Lord, happy is she.**
> **(Proverbs 16:20 NKJV)**

> The hard trek is past, friends. What a strenuous journey! We stroll easy slopes for the next few days and then home. Can't wait for you to discover the gift God lavishes on us today in the Meadow of Gladness.

Gladness emotes a sense of well-being and contentment, appreciation and quiet joy. Do you know this gladness is a gift from our Father God? One He wrapped up with a bow for you.

> Then I realized that it is good and proper for a man (woman) to eat and drink and to find satisfaction in his toilsome labor under the sun during the few days of life God has given him, for this is his lot. Moreover, when God gives any man (woman) wealth and possessions and enables him to enjoy them, to accept his lot and be happy in his work, this is a gift of God. He (She) seldom reflects on the days of his (her) life because God keeps him (her) occupied with *gladness of heart*.
> (Ecclesiastics 5:18–20)

Wow, did you catch it? God offers the gift of gladness during our ordinary days. Let's face it; many days are *not* filled with sorrows. They are *regular days*. Yet we succumb to feeling depressed, dispirited, irritable, just plain low. Definitely, not victorious Christians on those days. This scripture provides the antidote.

We eat and drink because we must, scarfing a burger on the run or dining at leisure. Diet manuals encourage us to serve an attractive plate, sit at a table, and eat slowly. Savoring your food satisfies your appetite. Eating slowly triggers a gratifying full sensation. Seeking joy and satisfaction in small moments of life cumulates in hours of gladness. It cultivates an attitude of thanksgiving and praise. Since we eat often, take a few seconds to savor, enjoy and find pleasure in what you consume. Try a simple, "Lord, thank you. This sandwich tastes so good."

Ok, lunch is over, back to work. Notice the scripture says, "Toilsome labor under the sun". Toilsome means full of long strenuous, fatiguing labor. Under the sun means hot, sweaty, and thirsty. Not a pretty picture, is it? Yet God's word says to find *satisfaction* even in strenuous, fatiguing labor. It continues, "for this is his/her lot." Oh, my goodness, I didn't want to hear that. If you are like me, you prefer easy labor for ample income. Characters on a 1980s TV episode of "Moonlighting" chanted marching around their desks, "No work with pay! No work with pay!" Unfortunately, not God's plan.

Hard work generates self-confidence, character, strength, motivation, satisfaction and ultimately our gladness of heart. However, since toilsome labor is arduous, to find satisfaction in it we must "accept our lot." Sometimes, we cannot transfer to a more enjoyable job. Perhaps, we have a good position yet find it stressful. We may not earn enough money to make ends meet. These are realistic dissatisfactions. Even so, I challenge you to accept that one must work (include child rearing) and affirm that God is in control. Now examine aspects for which you can be thankful. Hey, you have a job! That's a start. Do not gloss over wrongs or ignore stressful tasks at work, rather find satisfaction in accomplishment. Focus on the positive. Cultivate appreciation for your toilsome labor.

Moreover, when God gives any *woman* wealth and possessions and enables her to enjoy them, to accept her lot and be happy in her work, this is a gift of God.

We live in an affluent society. Most have "more than enough", beyond food, shelter and clothing. We buy flat-screen TV's, cell phones, vacations, and gel nails, yet we still complain. Oh yes, me too! Look at the next passage.

> I have seen another evil under the sun, and it weighs heavily on *women*. God gives a *woman* wealth, possessions, and honor, so that she lacks nothing her heart desires, but God does not enable her to enjoy them. This is meaningless, a grievous evil.
>
> (Ecclesiastics 6:1–2)

Lack of appreciation and enjoyment of God's provision, be it abundance or sustenance is a grievous evil. These are strong words. Compare a modest apartment with running water, heat and a toilet to the lives of our ancestors or those today under persecution or poverty. Everything above basic subsistence is wealth. Blessed with abundance, are we appreciative? Would you rather be dwelling on gladness of heart or pig manure?

> A sow that is washed goes back to her wallowing in the mud.
>
> (2 Peter 2:22)

Yuk! What a silly question! Of course, we prefer gladness of heart. Still, the human condition gravitates like the sow (female pig) back to the mud. "Lacking nothing" we continue to concentrate on what we *do not have*. How comforting the mud (complaining, disgruntlement, envy, accumulation) feels, yet how deceiving is this comfort. Pigs belong in the mud, not people. Yet like Paul in the "dodo" scriptures we flounder and like Paul "thanks be to God through Christ our Lord" we need not stay there.

> We know that the law is spiritual; but I am unspiritual, sold as a slave to sin. I do not understand what I do. For what I want to do I do not do, but what I hate I do. And if I do what I do not want to do, I agree that the law is good. As it is, it is no longer I myself who does it, but it is sin living in me. For I know that good itself does not dwell in me, that is, in my sinful nature. For I have the desire to do what is good, but I cannot carry it out. For I do not do the good I want to do, but the evil I do not want

to do—this I keep on doing. Now if I do what I do not want to do, it is no longer I who do it, but it is sin living in me that does it.

(Romans 7:14–29).

It is God who enables us to be content in our circumstances, to do what is good. It is His gift to us. Remember…

Moreover, when God gives any *woman* wealth and possessions and *enables her to enjoy* them, to accept her lot and be happy in her work, *this is a gift of God*.

No matter your paycheck, workload, or family responsibilities, ask *daily* for God's gift of gladness! Praise God for your physical circumstances, your possessions, your riches, as they are *right now*. So, you may say, "*She seldom reflects on the days of her life because God keeps her occupied with gladness of heart*".

> Gladness of heart is my favorite gift of God. I pray for it most every day, no matter the circumstances. Gladness flows when life is pleasant but extinguishes with a mere puff of hardship. Without His gift, the day is just a day, with His gift it is a celebration. Come along, women of God, He has a surprise for us along the trail.

Prayer: God of the Universe, Maker of Heaven and Earth, my Father and giver of wondrous gifts, we ask for your gift of gladness of heart to occupy our days. Give us eyes to see our abundance and be satisfied. Amen.

Hide in My Heart: "Then I realized that it is good and proper for a man (woman) to eat and drink and to find satisfaction in her toilsome labor under the sun during the few days of life God has given her, for this is her lot. Moreover, when God gives any woman wealth and possessions and enables her to enjoy them, to accept her lot and be happy in her work, this is a gift of God. She seldom reflects on the days of her life because God keeps her occupied with *gladness of heart*" (Ecclesiastic's 5:18–20).

Choose Today: As for me, I choose gladness that comes from God, not based on fickle circumstances.

Week 48, Day 2. Read: Colossians 3:23–24.
Journal: What dissatisfaction do you recite about your daily lot? How is your lot toilsome? Are you willing to receive His gift, or prefer to dwell in disgruntlement?
Action Tool: Pray for the gift of Gladness of Heart.

Week 48, Day 3. Read: Romans 7:14–8:11.
Journal: Do you find along with Paul that you do what you do not want to do? How so? What is the answer from Romans to Paul's question, "Who will rescue me?" Through what power?
Action Tool: Choose an attitude that hinders you from doing what you want to do. Write a "Put-Off" and a "Put-On" for this attitude. Agree with God that it needs to change.

Week 48, Day 4. Read: Luke 12:15–21, 1 John3:17–18.
Journal: What "wealth and possessions" has the lord provided you? Remember, everything over basic needs is wealth. How are you using your "riches" to bless others? Do you find contentment with your sustenance and possessions?
Action Tool: Walk around your "lands" (house, yard, garage, workplace, people, meals, everything) and note what you appreciate. Aim for a list of 100. Tuck this list in your Bible to review often.

Week 48, Day 5. Read: Ecclesiastics 5:18–20.
Journal: Does your mind become occupied with past regrets, hurts, or disappointments? God wants us to focus on today. How might today become more abundant for you?
Joy Trail: God gives gladness of heart to enable contentment amid our weary lot in life. Ask Him daily for this gift.

Heavenly Hot Springs
Week 49, Day 1

> Do you not know that your body is a temple of the Holy Spirit who is in you, whom you have received from God? You are not your own; you were bought at a price. Therefore, honor God with your body.
> (1 Corinthians 6:19–20)

Walk along these narrow boards, girlfriends, to a surprise. Tadah! The original Day Spa! God's natural hot springs flowing out of the ground at a perfect temperature to soak our weary bodies. Early pilgrims constructed the boardwalk and rock lined pool. Primitive but it does the trick.

God created an amazing earth! Pure water to drink and cleanse. Fruit and vegetables to nourish us. Majestic forests, woods and lakes to inspire us. Even kittens and puppies to kiss and cuddle. In addition, He created the first spa day. Hot springs to soak, soothe and heal. God is so good.

At a primitive Alaskan wilderness site in 1959, I first experienced hot springs. Skip forward 15 years to Hot Springs, Arkansas. The sign on a large plantation house claimed "Treatments, $15.00". Directed to a personal claw-foot tub, offered a cup of hot mineral water to drink, a good soak ensued. A massage and a cup of lemonade in a rocking chair followed. Take me back!

Why this discussion on hot springs? Our Lord provides care for our body and mind. The hot water soak was His idea. Make the health and well-being of your body a priority. This includes reducing stress that affects our physical well-being.

> Do you not know that your body is a temple of the Holy Spirit who is in you, whom you have received from

God? You are not your own; you were bought at a price. Therefore, honor God with your body.
>
> (1 Corinthians 6:19–20)

Upkeep of this temple includes refraining from immorality, trusting in God, eating healthy, exercise, and general maintenance of your mind and body. Visiting your own "Heavenly Hot Springs" will comfort during the stress of life. Think beyond pleasure, gals, which brings a high and then a crash. Think contentment, inspiration, awe and ahhh!

A quiet time of prayer, meditation, or contemplation restores our spiritual well-being and physical body. It alters the brains' neural pathways making one more resilient to stress. For those of us walking with our Savior, quiet time alone is a vital link to surrendering, resting, and rising refreshed. Find a moment or an hour every day for this "Joy Boost".

A diet of whole foods, complex carbohydrates, vegetables and non-processed foods encourages health. Consider an alternate comfort food when stress drives you towards a high sugar chocolate bar or a bag of potato chips. How about guacamole with bean chips or a frozen berry smoothie with a handful of almonds?

> Healthy foods that boost the feel-good hormones:
> Oatmeal Berries 9 Grain breads Quinoa Spinach Salmon Tea Pistachios Almonds Avocados Cheese Dark Chocolate Bananas

Exercise releases feel-good chemicals into the brain, therefore, go walking, biking, or stretch and do a few jumping jacks.

A hot soak has been a therapeutic remedy since God created hot springs, well-used by ancient Rome, the Vikings and American Indians. Even hot moist compresses are soothing to aching muscles. At home try lavender scented Epson salts in a hot bath. The magnesium sulfate in Epson salt absorbs through the skin relaxing muscles and increasing serotonin, the hormone that promotes a sense of well-being.

Time apart from daily life, a twenty-four hour get-away or a full vacation, has amazing health and stress releasing benefits. Vacations lower blood pressure, reduce the risk of heart disease, decrease stress and depression, foster creativity and create a more positive outlook on life. Just planning a vacation boosts your joy levels. If illness prevents good health, ask the Lord to reveal His best for you during that illness. Even in illness, the mind at rest with God fosters healing and well-being.

Quick "Joy Boosts" during your day:

1. Breathe deep—Sit still, eyes closed, feet on the floor, breathe in through your nose thinking "relax", breathe out through your mouth thinking, "Let go, rest in Jesus".
2. Laugh out loud—Watch something funny or just laugh alone in the car. Even faking a laugh increases the endorphins.
3. Sing out loud—Singing lowers blood pressure and anxiety. Play favorite music and sing heartily.
4. Dance—Play a favorite oldie and dance when no one is watching. Or join a dance exercise class.
5. Instant Vacation—Imagine your favorite place in the world. Be there in your mind.
6. Give someone a hug.
7. Give someone a compliment.
8. Call a friend.
9. Cuddle up with a book in cozy coffee shop.
10. Buy a smoothie and head to a park alone to walk and sip.
11. Invite a friend over for cookies and a cup of tea.
12. Dress pretty for no reason but to please yourself.
13. Get your hands in the dirt, plant a flower.
14. Light a candle with a wonderful aroma.
15. Indulge in your hobby.
16. Plan an adventure.
17. Play with a child or watch little children play.
18. Secretly do something nice.
19. Write a love letter and pop it in the mail.
20. Pet a dog or cat.
21. Go barefoot in the sand or grass.
22. Watch a sunset or get up early for a sunrise.
23. Walk in the rain.

24. Look at your schedule and cross off one less important task.
25. Focus on what is right rather than wrong, at this moment of your life.

> Pour me on the ground for a nap, gals. After that long soak, I'm not good for much else. My heart sings, "It is good to praise the LORD and make music to your name, O Most High, proclaiming your love in the morning and your faithfulness at night to the music of the ten-stringed lyre and the melody of the harp. For you make me glad by your deeds, LORD; I sing for joy at what your hands have done,"
>
> (Psalm 92: 1-4).

Prayer: My Lord, I surrender this body, mind and actions. Enable me to make choices which bring health and well-being to this temple. Amen.
Hide in My Heart: "Do you not know that your body is a temple of the Holy Spirit who is in you, whom you have received from God? You are not your own; you were bought at a price. Therefore, honor God with your body" (1 Corinthians 6:19–20).
Choose Today: I choose to honor God by caring for His temple, my body, mind, spirit and soul.

Week 49 Day 2. Read: 1 Corinthians 6: 12–20.
Journal: List how you dishonor God with your body. How does sexual immorality harm the temple? List how you care for your temple of God.
Action Tool: Choose 2 "Joy Boosts" to experience this week.

Week 49, Day 3. Read: Ephesians 5:15–20.
Journal: Pray for guidance on specific steps necessary for your physical well-being. Consider your health restrictions. Pray for power to implement and follow through with heathy choices. Note three steps to better health.
Action Tool: Take one step.

Week 49, Day 4. Read: Psalm 16.
Journal: "Rest in Jesus" by setting aside time for your own private spa day. Include moment to sit quiet, walk, talk, dance and sing with the Lord. Describe this day. The goal is "Ahhh".
Action Tool: Write on your calendar appointments for…

a. Quiet contemplation with the Lord
b. Physical exercise
c. Your personal "Spa Day".

If not scheduled, it won't happen.

Week 49, Day 5. Read: Matthew 11:28–29.
Journal: Remember to nourish your mind, body and soul. What part is most neglected? What can you do to change this? How is God working in you in these areas?
Action Tool: Create a "Joy Board". Collect pictures of things, thoughts, dreams, scriptures, activities which bring you joy. These can be photos, or magazine pages, scribbles, or random words. Paste them on a piece of cardboard. Go crazy with a collage. Glance at the collage everyday praising God.
Joy Trail: Play uplifting music and sing aloud. Dance around the room alone. Grab the kids and dance with them.

A Cup of Cool Water
Week 50, Day 1

And if anyone gives even a cup of cold water to one of these little ones who is my disciple, truly I tell you, that person will certainly not lose their reward.

(Matthew 10:42)

> After the hot springs, we crave a long cold drink. Jennifer, your purifier is handy. Let's purify water from this fast-flowing creek. Kara, your face is flushed. Would you like a cup of cool water?

God is calling. He is asking us to give a "cup of cold water" to someone who is thirsty. Stuck in the everyday tread mill of family and work, we may not notice our friend or coworker who needs a little tender care. Yet being the cup bearer quickens joy. God admonishes us not to ignore the need of others.

> For I was hungry, and you gave me something to eat, I was thirsty, and you gave me something to drink, I was a stranger and you invited me in, I needed clothes and you clothed me, I was sick, and you looked after me, I was in prison and you came to visit me.
> Then the righteous will answer him, "Lord, when did we see you hungry and feed you, or thirsty and give you something to drink? When did we see you a stranger and invite you in, or needing clothes and clothe you? When did we see you sick or in prison and go to visit you?"
> The King will reply, "Truly I tell you, whatever you did for one of the least of these brothers and sisters of mine, you did for me."
>
> (Matthew 25: 35–40)

"But," you say, "I am overwhelmed. Isn't being a slave to my family enough? Why are you piling more on me?" Hey, calm down now. Serving with your special talents will activate *more joy*, not stress. Before you were born, God appointed you to carry out certain good works. Open your mind and be aware. God will reveal "cup of cold-water moments".

> For we are God's handiwork, created in Christ Jesus to do good works, which God prepared in advance for us to do.
> (Ephesians 2:10)

He calls some to teach Sunday school, host Bible studies, visit convalescent homes, take part in church children's clubs, short-term missionary work, crisis pregnancy, or gospel missions. Christian programs need many helpers. God inspires service with love, not guilt. He will:

a. Place a burden on your heart for the ministry.
b. Give you a desire and a willingness to serve.
c. Show you how to carve out time for this service.
d. Bless as you minister in his name.

This book, <u>A Daily Walk to Joy in the Midst,</u> lay in thought many years. God gave me the burden and desire to write. Still, time for this project seemed nonexistent. I felt guilty and disobedient. Finally, I surrendered and relaxed. I would wait for Him to appoint the time in my life.

> The one who calls you is faithful, and he will do it.
> (1 Thessalonians 5:24)

> Being confident of this, that he who began a good work in you will carry it on to completion until the day of Christ Jesus.
> (Philippians 1:6)

About ten years passed. Then a few years ago, my husband announced it was time. I couldn't get started. My jumble of notes and journals had no cohesiveness. My husband encouraged me to spend a week alone with God. While grumbling I would be lonely, the Lord spoke to my heart. This was

His appointed time. My Abba Father strolled the beach with me inspiring, guiding and providing insight beyond my abilities. Amazing!

> There is a time for everything, and a season for every activity under the heavens.
>
> (Ecclesiastes 3:1)

During busy seasons of life, many moments are available to *give a cup of cold water*. In the morning, ask the Lord to reveal someone who needs a moment of your time, a God ordained appointment. When the moment comes, the Holy Spirit convicts and guides. Delight in discovering these "cup of cold water" opportunities to serve.

> Do not withhold good to those from whom it is due when it is in your power to act.
>
> (Proverbs 3:27)

Here are a few moments God appointed for me last year:

- ❖ Being a secret sister to a suffering friend. Sending her little gifts and cards of encouragement for a time. Finally, inviting her to lunch to meet the anonymous secret sister.
- ❖ Handing a Kleenex to a woman who was crying in an airport and saying, "I will pray for you." She responded with a hug.
- ❖ Giving a shuffling elder lady who had walked to a store and now seemed lost, a ride back home.
- ❖ Lingering with the owner of a shoe store, whom I barely knew, as she closed for the night. Her husband died two weeks earlier, so she cried and reminisced over the store opening thirty-eight years before.
- ❖ Dropping off flowers from my garden to a friend.

You get the idea. Many opportunities occur to share a word of God, pray, offer help or encouragement. All are "cups of cold water" that will strengthen your heart. No guilt trip here. Be aware. Be ready, then wait and watch for your God appointments.

> Ahhh, this water is so good. I feel refreshed. It is only a couple miles to our last campsite. Don your packs for the final push.

Prayer: We know you give us "cup of cold water" assignments, Lord. Motivate us to listen and act instead of ignoring those nudges. To Him be the glory. Amen.

Hide in My Heart: "Truly I tell you, whatever you did for one of the least of these brothers and sisters of mine, you did for me," (Matthew 25:40)

Choose Today: I choose to be available for "God Appointments" in the midst of my day. Lord, set them up as you see fit.

Week 50, Day 2. Read: Matthew 25:35–40.
Journal: How is this scripture speaking to you? What restrains you from spontaneous following of the Holy Spirit.
Action Tool: Volunteer to serve for an outreach event by your church or community.

Week 50, Day 3. Read: Ephesians 2:4–10.
Journal: Ask the Lord to highlight God Appointments for you. Pray for confirmation, courage and boldness as you step out in response to His nudges.
Action Tool: Watch for a God appointment.

Week 50, Day 4. Read: Philippians 1:6.
Journal: Is being open to serve "resting in Jesus" or a guilt trip for you? How are the results different if we serve out of our own strength instead of God's calling? Does serving because God empowers us mean it will be easy? If serving creates hardship are you still willing? Why or why not?
Action Tool: Watch for a God appointment.

Week 50, Day 5. Read: Ecclesiastes 3:1–14.
Journal: What tasks occupy your time during this season of your life? Are there "cup of cold water" opportunities? Ponder His calling to you for this season.

Action Tool: On trips with your children or spouse, before you start the car, pray for "God Sightings." These are moments when you see "God at work" or "God speaking or motivating". Share these sightings at dinner that night.

Joy Trail: As you volunteer to help another, your own sorrow will disappear (even if only for a moment). Give of yourself in a way you enjoy.

Lake of Still Waters
Week 51, Day 1

A cheerful heart is good medicine.
(Proverbs 17:22a)

> Well, my dear journey friends, you finished the trek! Welcome to my favorite meadow in the entire world by the Lake of Still Waters. Shed your packs and celebrate! Our Lord walked with us each day whether or not we were aware of him. He guided our footsteps, protecting us and restoring our soul. "He leadeth me beside still waters, He restoreth my soul,
>
> (Psalm 23:2 KJV)."

Because of our pain and His love, we earnestly sought our God. Our minds accepted His conviction and correction. We listened for his still small voice. Leaning on the everlasting arms for strength, we applied His teaching to our life. We are more than conquerors through Christ Jesus.

> His master replied, 'Well done, good and faithful servant! You have been faithful with a few things; I will put you in charge of many things. Come and share your master's happiness!
>
> (Matthew 25:21)

Though we completed one phase, the journey through life continues. Expect more trials and pain yet ahead. Loved ones will need our sacrifice and forgiveness. We will feel confused, lost and alone. We live in a fallen world, so no individual person and no circumstance guarantees contentment and restoration, only God. God will be ever present for you. He is waiting, every day, always patient for you, only you.

> You did not choose me, but I chose you and appointed you so that you might go and bear fruit—fruit that will last—and so that whatever you ask in my name the Father will give you.
>
> (John 15:16)

He will never lose a single one of us who call upon his name…

> And this is the will of him who sent me that I shall lose none of all those he has given me but raise them up at the last day.
>
> (John 6:39)

> For I am convinced that neither death nor life, neither angels nor demons, neither the present nor the future, nor any powers, neither height nor depth, nor anything else in all creation, will be able to separate us from the love of God that is in Christ Jesus our Lord.
>
> (Romans 8:38–39)

And in the end, he will take you home with him…

> Do not let your hearts be troubled. You believe in God; believe also in me. My Father's house has many rooms; if that were not so, would I have told you that I am going there to prepare a place for you? And if I go and prepare a place for you, I will come back and take you to be with me that you also may be where I am.
>
> (John 14:1–3)

He is for us. He is our God! Our Jesus! Our Lord! He has promised us…

> Peace, I leave with you; my peace I give you. I do not give to you as the world gives. Do not let your hearts be troubled and do not be afraid.
>
> (John 14:27)

> I have told you these things, so that in me you may have peace. In this world you will have trouble. But take heart! I have overcome the world.
>
> (John 16:33)

> Pilgrims, we have traveled over the Mountain of Gloom to the Lake of Still Waters. It hasn't been easy, but I have seen each of you grow in perseverance and maturity. My soul thrills for the faith I see shining out of your faces. Rejoice tonight as we gather one last time around the campfire. "Oh, Lord my God, as I in awesome wonder consider all the worlds thy hands have made. Then sings my soul, my savior God to thee, how great thou art, how great thou art."
>
> How Great Thou Art, Stuart K Hine, b. 1899

Prayer: Lord, all we have, all we are, is yours. Though we live in the world, we are not of the world. Protect us from the evil-one, sanctify us by the truth of your word. You are our joy. True gladness of heart comes from leaning on You. Amen.

Hide in My Heart: "For I am convinced that neither death nor life, neither angels nor demons, neither the present nor the future, nor any powers, neither height nor depth, nor anything else in all creation, will be able to separate us from the love of God that is in Christ Jesus our Lord" (Romans 8:38–39)

Choose Today: I am confident that nothing can separate me from the love of God that is in Christ Jesus our Lord.

Week 51, Day 2. Read: John 15:16, John 6:39 and Romans 8:38–39.
Journal: Looking back over the year, review changes God enabled in your life. Review failures. What problems still exist? Does God the Father, Son and Holy Spirit sometimes still feel far away? Doubts may linger. After a whole year of concentrating on walking with God, it can be discouraging. Journal how today's scriptures address these issues.
Action Tool: Through the years ahead during times of doubt, remember to say, "I believe, help me overcome my unbelief" (Matthew 9:24).

Week 51, Day 3. Read: Ephesians 2:1–8 and John 14:2–3.
Journal: We may fear that something we do or have done will lose our salvation? Write Ephesians 2:8 in your journal. What does scripture clearly conclude regarding your salvation?
Action Tool: If trusting in your salvation is an issue for you, write 10 times, "I am confident that nothing can separate me from the love of God that is in Christ Jesus our Lord."

Week 51, Day 4. Read: James 1:22; Galatians 5:5, 7, 13–14, 22–25.
Journal: Why have you spent a whole year putting your faith into action? How has focusing on the admonitions of the Lord drawn you closer to Him? What is His call to you going forward?
Action Tool: Sing a love song to the Lord.

Week 51, Day 5. Read: John 14:27 and John 16:33.
Journal: Journal how you have experienced God's peace amid your struggles over this past year.
Action Tool: Write a psalm of praise for the goodness of God to you. Hint: Choose a psalm (perhaps Psalm 98 or 100) to paraphrase. Write your own praises and exultations.

Happy Trails to You, Until We Meet Again
Week 52, Day 1

> **Trust in the Lord with all your heart and lean not on your own understanding; in all your ways submit to him, and he will make your paths straight.**
> **(Proverbs 3:5–6)**

> Arise, sisters, the outfitters will be here soon to carry us to our cars. Back to real life, but never alone. We have our God, our Jesus, and each other. I tucked a note into your packs last night. God's heart for you. Find a quiet place to savor His words before we break camp.

My Dear Daughter,

My grace is sufficient for you, (no matter how you might feel today), for my power is made perfect in your weakness.* Since you have been justified through faith, you have peace with God through our Lord Jesus Christ, through whom you have gained access by faith into this grace in which you now stand. And you can boast in the hope of the glory of God. Not only so, but you also can glory in your sufferings, because you know that suffering produces perseverance; perseverance, character; and character hope. And hope does not put you to shame, because God's love

---

* 2 Corinthians 12:9

has been poured out into your heart through the Holy Spirit, who has been given to you.*

I pray that out of his glorious riches he may strengthen you with power through his Spirit in your inner being, so that Christ may dwell in your heart through faith. And I pray that you, being rooted and established in love, may have power, together with all the Lord's holy people, to grasp how wide and long and high and deep is the love of Christ, and to know this love that surpasses knowledge – that you may be filled to the measure of all the fullness of God.**

Forever,
Your Loving Father

---

* Romans 5:1–5
** Ephesians 3:16–19.

Epilogue

Having shared with you about the struggles, I am thrilled to also share some of the miracles. True moments of God's intervention.

Lost in the mountains, back-packing with my eleven-year-old niece, I prayed, "God show us the way." Into my mind and out of my mouth popped, "God said he will lead us down the mountain and has prepared a fire, dinner and place to sleep." Immediately, after speaking to my niece, thoughts came into my head, "Now, you've done it. When this doesn't happen, she will never believe in God." Then I turned and saw the cairns mentioned in "Abba's Trail" and a broken trail sign. Following the steep trail darkness engulfed us. My niece complained of weariness and hunger. Finally, we rounded huge boulders at the edge of the lake. Two college men called to us, "Hey, we saw you up on that cliff earlier. Come on over, we have a fire, food and a place to sleep ready for you." Amazing!

When in Romania to adopt my daughter, my mother and I encountered many obstacles, yet God became so real. Like holding Daddy's hand. I woke up saying, "OK, Daddy, what do we do today?" Then Our Rescuer showed me the next step to rescue my child from the orphanage. This powerful experience cemented our belief in the adoption being God's will. Even when troubles occurred at home with our daughter, we never doubted.

Our nine-year-old son felt abandoned when his mother, me, brought home an out of control sister after being gone for three months. Up to that time, he was an only child. Now, Mom was preoccupied with a daughter who knew nothing about living in a family. Michael felt ignored. Our home life was crazy. Despite this Michael continued to grow in the Lord, to become a fine and stable young man. Through his doubts, he emerged to continue his walk with God. Given our dysfunctional home and lack of focus on his needs, our son could have gone far astray. Our God was faithful to our son!

Monica, when she arrived, was super disruptive. Then one day when she was eight, she said to her Dad, "I don't want to be like this anymore!" Gene told her, "Well Jesus can heal you. All you need to do is ask him into your heart." "Ok, Daddy, I want to do it." So right there in the car on the way to the hardware store, Monica prayed to ask Jesus into her heart. Immediately, all destructive behaviors ceased! For the next three years, Monica was a typical strong-willed child but amazingly wholesome! When she entered puberty, hormones ignited bad behaviors which catapulted us into several years of extreme situations. However, God provided Christian mentors for Monica through every step bringing her through those troubled years to be a fine woman today.

Gene, my prince turned ogre turned beloved, reads the Bible every day and turns me to the Lord when I am discouraged. He sought council when needed. My husband once full of critical remarks, has become my greatest fan and support in my endeavors. Gene is still intense, opinionated and prone to depression, yet his heart belongs to God and to me. That two people who wanted a divorce after their honeymoon could become one of heart and mind is a major miracle!

Recently, our new daughter, Danielle, wife of our Michael, was an answer to years of prayer. Ages ago, when she and Michael were just friends at work, I began praying for her. She was not a believer yet searching. My prayer was, "Lord, meet Danielle along the way and introduce her to our Jesus." I never shared this with Danielle. When Danielle was in Taiwan for a year teaching English, I received an email from her, "Anne, what do you think about this? I was riding my bicycle to work when I felt like God was speaking to me. 'Hey, Danielle, you need to know my son Jesus.'" During that season in Taiwan she became a believer in Jesus.

God is awesome! Many more "God Sightings" happened in our daily life. He has blessed us abundantly with joy in the midst. May it always be so with you as well.

> Journey Partners, Women of God, remember, Jesus said, "In this world you shall have tribulation, but be of good cheer, I have overcome the world." And, so have you, Pilgrims. Choosing to be content and trust in God is the beginning and the end for a life of joy. I will pray for you, dear ones. Love, Anne

> Then we cried to the Lord in our trouble,
> and he saved us from our distress.
> He sent out his word and healed us;
> he rescued us from the grave.
> Let us give thanks to the Lord for his unfailing love
> and his wonderful deeds for mankind.
> Let us sacrifice thank offerings
> and tell of his works with songs of joy.
> (Psalm 107:19–22)

Hide in My Heart: "Trust in the Lord with all your heart and lean not on your own understanding; in all your ways submit to him, and he will make your paths straight" (Proverbs 3: 5–6).
Choose Today: For I will yet praise Him, my Lord and my God.

Week 52, Day 2. Read: 2 Corinthians 12:9, Romans 5:1-5, Romans 8:29, Ephesians 3:14–19.
Journal: Biblical Definition of Grace Encompasses: Loving kindness, mercy, forgiveness, salvation, regeneration, repentance and the love of God for us. Devine power equips man/woman to live a moral life. Journal your thoughts.
Action Tool: Be still and know I am God. Sit still and rejoice in the work of the Holy Spirit transforming you into a woman of grace.

Week 52, Day 3. Read: Reread John Chapters 13.
Journal: Journal your thoughts.
Action Tool: Write and post this affirmation, "I am loved by God. I am of great value in his eyes. I am His. Through his strength within me, and for the joy before me, I give my day to Him." Read it every morning before you brush your teeth.

Week 52, Day 4. Read: Reread John Chapters 15:1–17.
Journal: Journal your thoughts.
Action Tool: Choose a life verse that speaks to your heart and soul. Write and post it on your car visor. Read it every day before you start the engine.

Week 52, Day 5. Read: Psalm 27:13–14
Journal: Write out your hope for the new year walking with God.
Joy Trail: Claim hope. The story isn't over yet. Affirm that you will yet praise him, your God and Savior. You are living in the joy of the Lord. Amen.

Note from the Author

Thank you, Journey Friends, for giving me
the opportunity to share with you.

Since writing this book, time marches along giving me two
grandsons and four grand girls to spoil. Life is full, yet even
now I must daily seek God's grace, peace, and healing,
letting go if issues out of my control and resting in my Lord.
Never give up Lady Friends. God is so good. Amen

Guidelines for Group Study

Joy in the Midst Discussion and Prayer Support Group

Women need comfort, support, encouragement, and action to grow and thrive amid life's trials. A Daily Walk to Joy in the Midst was written for that purpose. Here are some general guidelines to assist in using the book for a small group. Time commitment for each woman is 10 to 15 minutes a day, 5 days a week, plus 1 ½ hour discussion and prayer weekly.

1. This gathering has no teacher, rather a discussion facilitator. Her purpose is to ensure everyone has an opportunity to share, and no one monopolizes the conversation (including the leader). Start and close the study on time. Ask the questions. Set aside a half hour for prayer.
2. Follow the 52-week lessons for 5 days each week. It is OK to start with Lesson 1 anytime during the year or to take more than a year to finish. Do not meet on holiday weeks.
3. During the week, participants read the sections and scriptures. Each sister does the homework as she feels led, no pressure.
4. Come together as a group 1 ½ hour per week. Allow time for visiting after study, perhaps with cookies and coffee.
5. Open the study with prayer and scripture memory recitation.
6. Discussion (Same questions each week):
    a. From this week's lesson, how did the Lord speak to your heart?
    b. What emotions or circumstances did it bring up?
    c. Did you apply an action tool? What effect did it have for you?
    d. What nugget will you embrace going forward from this week?
7. Spend the last half hour praying for concerns shared during discussion.